Disability and Impairment

Disability and Impairment
Working with Children and Families

Peter Burke

Jessica Kingsley Publishers
London and Philadelphia

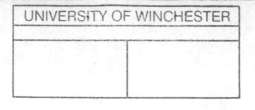

First published in 2008
by Jessica Kingsley Publishers
116 Pentonville Road
London Nl 9JB, UK
and
400 Market Street, Suite 400
Philadelphia, PA 19106, USA

www.jkp.com

Library of Congress Cataloging in Publication Data
Burke, Peter (Peter C.)
    Disability and impairment : working with children and families / Peter Burke. -- 1st
American paperback ed.
        p. cm.
    Includes bibliographical references.
    ISBN 978-1-84310-396-7 (pb : alk. paper) 1. Social work with children with disabilities.
2. Children with disabilities--Family relationships. I. Title.
    HV888.B87 2008
    362.4--dc22

                                                                2007033243

British Library Cataloguing in Publication Data
A CIP catalogue record for this book is available from the British Library

ISBN 978 1 84310 396 7

Printed and bound in Great Britain by
Athenaeum Press, Gateshead, Tyne and Wear

Contents

Figures

Tables

Acknowledgements: A Professional and Personal Dedication

I would like to dedicate this book to those people and organisations that provided the opportunity to undertake a series of research studies that made the text possible. I remain grateful to the source funding provided by the Children's Research Fund, the Nuffield Foundation, and funding derived, via the University of Hull, from the Higher Education Funding Council in England; without financial input and encouragement during the initial stages of investigation the research could not have been completed. I was fortunate to be supported by three colleagues, Katy Cigno, Sue Montgomery and Ben Fell, who were employed at different times as research assistants and this is reflected in the publication of various reports as the research progressed and developed.

However, the book would not have been written at all if my son, a previously healthy and lively child, had not, following treatment to cure leukaemia at the age of three in 1989, acquired severe brain injury, leaving him spastic–quadriplegic. This encounter with disability changed the life of my family. Further, my daughter, born during the time of her brother's treatment, later reflected a caring attitude towards her brother which inspired the fieldwork for the book *Brothers and Sisters of Disabled Children* (Burke 2004). Her younger brother was born three months prematurely in November 1990. He, at the age of 18 months, was diagnosed with spastic diplegia, and at the time of writing uses a powered wheelchair to enable his mobility. My family experience motivated my research interest in understanding the situation of other families living with childhood disability.

My personal dedication is to my family, Heather my partner, and our children, Marc, Sammy and Joe.

Introduction

This book examines the role of the professional in assisting families with a disabled child. It also considers the needs of siblings with disabled brothers and sisters and, of course, the needs of the disabled child. The book is about the context of disability in the family. It shows how the experience of living with a disabled child becomes a 'family matter'. The issues faced by disabled people of all ages within the family context are debated within a needs framework based on the social model of disability. The model is utilised as a building block for considering the associative conditions of disability which impact on all family members. The impact of disability on others helps to provide a holistic view of disability in its many manifestations, restrictions and experience of social exclusion.

The structure of the book

The book is structured around a number of theoretical perspectives on disability, impairment and experiences of disability in the family. It draws on evidence from four research projects, all of which point towards a need for a family view of disability. The book consists of nine chapters, with practice notes at the end of each chapter to guide the reader through a number of key themes as they are introduced. An Appendix gives insights into the research process.

Chapter 1 explores the theory of disability and impairment, together with medical and social models of disability. The family context of disability is also examined.

In Chapter 2, an associative model of disability is outlined to show how all family members are involved when a child of the family is discovered to be disabled. The conceptual understanding of stigma is examined to show how it links to the experience families encounter when confronted by differing attitudes towards disability.

Chapters 3 and 4 examine the impact of childhood disability. Chapter 3 presents the family viewpoint as reported by parents. Chapter 4 shows how professional social care workers need to focus on the family in order to understand how they initially react to disability, and how to identify appropriate service provision.

In Chapter 5 the issues of life transitions are addressed through a disabled child's progression from dependency to independence. This includes the experience of utilising sitter services, school and respite care, all part of a developmental process which enables parents and siblings to understand that a disabled child also makes choices and has a right to independence.

Chapter 6 is about sibling experiences. It draws from two of the author's research studies to show that disability by association is a useful way of understanding part of a sibling's identity in a family with a disabled child.

Chapter 7 reflects in the views of a group of young disabled people drawn from a study. Chapter 8 compares the benefits of group experiences for siblings and young people from the same group to suggest common elements in group processes which achieved successful outcomes for the young people involved.

Chapter 9 brings together the evidence to reflect on the role of family assessment when a child in the family has a disability, and makes recommendations for improving practice.

The insights offered in this book will be useful for those working with disability, living with disability, and teaching in matters related to disability. The text is informed, wherever possible, by quotations from the respondents involved to identify commonly expressed needs and concerns. Case studies of the lives of families and their children feature throughout to identify the reality of their experiences.

The author's intention is that this book should both clarify and offer an understanding of disability. It is to be hoped that our mutual understanding will be improved by considering not only our own reactions but also those of others who are involved, while at the same time attempting to make a positive difference to the families concerned.

Chapter 1

Disability and Impairment: Theory and Practice

This book is grounded in the reflective experiences of families who participated in research undertaken by the author. It will be seen that disability does actually define individuals in both positive and negative ways and that the issues this raises need to be debated. It is clear, too, that disability should not be the only defining element of the individual, who should define himself or herself and be accepted as such.

The issues faced by disabled people of all ages within the family context are examined here from a needs perspective supported by the social model of disability. The social model is viewed as a social construction, and the overarching need is to do something to ensure that disabled people do not experience encounters that reinforce a sense of disability. Consequently, disability needs a greater social acceptance and the research reported in this text points towards a way of achieving that objective, here with particular reference to child disability. In the familial acceptance of disability, cited research studies will show that the experience of disability transcends the individual with disability and partly becomes the property of siblings, parents and other family members. The professional role requires an understanding of such family matters.

The concept of *exclusion* will be introduced in explaining social reactions to disability and families living with disability who find their lives limited in various ways. This is also about the incapacity of individuals to control their lives, and the need to provide an opportunity 'to develop their potential' (Morris 2001, p.162). It is *not* about disability as a problem; it is about making disability accepted and understood.

Defining disability and impairment

The terms *disability* and *impairment* were chosen deliberately for the title of this book. They mean different things. It is easy to confuse the two, in the sense that an impairment may have a disabling effect. However, their use here will clarify the meanings of disability and impairment and so reduce any potential for confusion between the two terms. Exploring this will also enable a better understanding of their usage and application in professional practice.

Disability is viewed as some limitation imposed mainly by social experiences and opportunities that restrict an individual's ability to engage with others or to access specific locations. This view of disability sees it equating with the experience of 'social exclusion', where the perceived disability, due to imposed social barriers, effectively denies opportunity to participate and be involved with others. Impairment, on the other hand, is centred more on the individual, reflecting a type of functional difference when one person is compared with another. As Oliver (1996, p.13) clarified in talking about loss, disability is more about the comparative loss of opportunity in social settings, possibly through deliberate exclusion, whereas an impairment is an actual loss through an injury, illness or congenital condition. The former is more about attitudes and location, an external reality, compared with the latter which is more about an individual's physical and intellectual debility, an internal effect.

Barnes and Mercer (2003, p.66) reflect on the separation of impairment from disability using UPIAS (Union of Physically Impaired Against Segregation) and the Disabled People's International (DPI 1982) representations to explain that an impairment is a medical or professional determination of a 'bio-physiological limitation'. Thus, an impairment exhibits a physical and/or intellectual difficulty rather than a limitation imposed by an external source, as might be experienced in a social setting. Alternatively, disability, as referred to by Thomas (1999, p.39), is about restrictions of activity that result from social experiences; and although an aspect of illness and impairment are disabling, disability as a social obstruction is not the same as an impairment.

'Impairment', to clarify the term, is to do with individual differences in functional activities, usually related to a 'diagnostic difference'. Examples might include experience with visual or hearing impairment, intellectual impairment to signify learning disability, or something personal that creates a difficulty in doing things that others may take for granted. Any manifestation of physical, intellectual and social restrictions needs to be minimised if not eliminated to reduce the social consequences of defining an individual's disability. An impairment will remain as a condition understood by the individual who may take measures to reduce its impact, or choose not to do so.

However, 'disability' tends to be the generalised term that is more often used, and so it is in this text; although, in reviewing models of disability, an understanding of impairment helps locate the disabled person between the medical and social models of disability, described in Burke (1993) as a person-centred approach. Consequently, the term 'disability' will appear as the overarching word inclusive of impairment and learning difficulties, underpinned by this conceptual distinction between disability and impairment.

Models of disability

According to Gillespie-Sells and Campbell (1991) the medical model of disability views disability as a condition to be cured. This is hardly surprising; the mainstay of medical training is about preventive treatment or curing illness, so a pathological orientation is to be expected. It is from such an idealised position that a person with a disability is viewed as someone needing treatment. Treatment is typically based on symptoms of illness which, according to Penn (2005), often means administering a drug, surgery or even palliative care. However, if an individual is considered only in treatment terms the pathological overrides the individual's sense of being. The person is objectified as though identified more with a condition, whether that is a diagnosed medical condition or, indeed, a clarification of a disability.

Thurgate and Warner (2005) comment on the difficulty of the medical model to incorporate the non-medical impact of living in disadvantaged conditions. They suggest that assumptions may be made about the level of disability experienced by the individual when, in fact, the disability is actually a reflection of the social environment. Clearly, individuals exist beyond the limitations of their diagnosed medical conditions, and it is recognising that sphere of relationships which helps define the individual and the need for a medical diagnosis. Indeed, in determining the impact of disability it is the social model of disability which aids our understanding of the cumulative effects on the individual of encounters with the medical profession and social experiences alike.

A social model indicates that disability is exacerbated by environmental factors and consequently the context of disability extends beyond the individual. Physical and social barriers may contribute to the perceived disability experienced by the individual (Swain *et al.* 2004). Questions may be asked, following the suggestions of Oliver (1990), such as 'What external factors should be changed to improve this person's situation?' For example, the need for attendance at a special school might be questioned if there is a more inclusive alternative within the locality, rather than assuming that the child with a disability *must* attend a special school. This is like saying that a disabled person must be monitored by a consultant rather than visiting a general practitioner when needing to do so. Consequently, in the school example, mainstream education might be preferable for many or most children with disabilities, but it is only viable if accompanied by participative policies of inclusion, encouragement for the child at school, and classroom support.

The social model should promote the needs of the individual within a community context such that the individual does not experience social exclusion because of his or her condition. In the example given, rather than withdrawing the child from the everyday experiences of others, integrated education would mean that he or she is part of the mainstream: it is a kind of normalisation process. The social model simply encourages changes to be made to the social setting so that the disabled individual is not disadvantaged by situational, emotional or physical barriers to access. Banks (1991) suggests that cultural misunderstanding is created by a sense of difference between minority groups attempting to exist within a dominant culture. Goodley (2000, p.36) proposed an inclusive social model of disability which, in relation to learning difficulties, recognises the social origins of 'learning difficulties' and 'difference', as indicating attitudinal reactions, but suggesting that whatever the causation of such difference, distinctions are not necessarily made in all cultures. Yang and McMullen (2003) show that learning about the culture of others may help us to improve our understanding of cultural differences with the implicit assumption that disabilities should not equate the term 'disability' with 'less able' in our society.

Models of disability seek to explain disability as a consequence of social experience, where social interactions between individuals transmute an impairment into a barrier which makes people with an impairment feel a greater sense of being disabled due to their treatment by others. The experience of *socially constructed disability* that results suggests that disabled people are subject to oppression by non-disabled people (Shakespeare and Watson 2002). This means that the disadvantage of disability arises from the unequal status that disabled people experience. The types of disadvantage experienced by disabled people also include restrictions imposed by access difficulties. An example that illustrates this most simply is that of the wheelchair user who cannot use a building due to the steps that have to be negotiated, an experience encountered by the author (Burke 2004, p.129). In such a situation, the steps reinforce an identity as disabled, whereas ramped access would not. It is clear that the way individuals interact in everyday life, where attitudes define disability through the process of stigmatisation mentioned earlier, or where access is problematic, all serve to reinforce a sense of disability for the individual with an impairment.

The medical model is criticised for its representation of an unequal power relationship between the professional and service user. Furthermore, it continues to 'objectify' disability and has the same pervasive problems as the individual model of impairment. The social model is criticised for its neglect of impairment at an individual level (Read 2000). According to Crow (1996, p.216), the social model is flawed because it appears to determine disability by a mainstream response, such that the sense of the individual with an impairment is lost. The medical model can be seen as taking power away from the person with the disability because those requiring treatment necessarily view doctors as possessors of medical knowledge, and consequently patients may succumb to medical authority. However, such views neglect the power of explanation of the social model, which defines disability by social actions; impairment is an individual experience, 'disability' is a restriction imposed by attempts at social engagement. The need is to incorporate both views, recognising the level of impairment and minimising social restrictions rather than assuming one is correct and the other is not.

The sense that the medical world is concerned with diagnosis and treatment does not auger well for those whose condition is not curable. The pathology of a medical condition, in a sense, overtakes the human condition, so the discussion of need concerns health status and symptoms rather than the individual. Largely, this is inevitable. It would be foolish to maintain that doctors and professions allied to medicine do not have an important part to play in learning disabled children's lives or that medicine should not be about diagnosis and treatment: we all have need of these skills and knowledge at some point in our lives.

The social context is crucial, therefore, for an understanding of individual needs and social interactions. Medical conditions should not get in the way of attending to individual social needs. In proposing an integrated approach in Burke and Cigno (2000), the attempt was to represent elements from both the medical and social worlds. The medical need is properly recognised in understanding the impact of impairments on the individual; but so is the social world, where the context of living with an impairment necessarily incorporates interactions of a social type, recognising and acting on any restrictions that this might impose.

The balance between the medical and the social has to be right. Recognising the contribution of different professional involvements helps that understanding. These issues are more easily addressed in multi-agency settings. A multi-agency approach, especially where medical, educational and social welfare professionals work under one roof and undertake multidisciplinary assessments, is one way forward.

Community care

At any one time, up to 1.5 million of the most vulnerable people in society are relying on social workers and support staff for help. Social care services also make a major contribution to tackling social exclusion (DoH 2007). The sense of community care is simple enough; the community should help with the care needs of its members. But simplicity was never the arbiter of practice, so it took the Griffiths Report (Griffiths 1988) and the NHS and Community Care Act 1990 to emphasise the need for care in the community with the suggestion that meeting needs rather than fitting people to available resources should be the way to provide services.

The problem is that resourcing those needs becomes an issue, so any suggestion about meeting wholesale needs is doomed if needs become an escalation of 'wants' rather than what is reasonable provision. The issue is that a principle-based vision of meeting needs clashes with a resource manager in control of finite resources. At some point the two are in conflict; that may vary from providing simple resources like a 'bath aid' or the refinements of some major adaptation to a service user's home. It seems that care and services can, for some, if not all, only result in a sense of failure to meet community needs.

When identifying a 'cycle' to this process (Burke and Cigno 1996, p.26) the situation of someone needing residential care is exemplified. The need for care in the community is potentially in conflict with the need for residential care in the community. This may be more familiar with the needs of older people when some become less able to manage their own care needs; but it is also a feature of the needs of young people with profound disabilities if and when their families cannot manage to provide the necessary care at home. When care is provided within the family home, and the family is meeting the care needs of an individual, that cannot and should not be called community care (whereby the community provides for care needs), although it *is* 'care in the community' because the family is living in the community. The reality may well be that care in the family home lacks a community identity, and community care would involve carers assisting with the care needs of the family.

The ethos of provision of care for the community is a failure in terms of the policy intent, particularly relating to the needs of disabled children. Community identities should be prescriptive to individual choice and lifestyle. The intent must be that social care services meet the proposals of the Green Paper *Every Child Matters*, now implemented in the Children Act 2004. This puts children first when supporting families, a message promoted earlier in Utting (1995) which identifies the legal duty of cooperation required in meeting child and family needs for short and longer-term needs. The latter utilises a Common Assessment Framework for Children and Young People (Department for Education and Skills (DfES) 2006, p.2) across the professions involved in social care.

Assessing the needs of children with disabilities

The study of prevalence of disability in children and young people, according to the National Statistics (2004), lacks accurate and good quality data at a national level so it is difficult to establish any clear long-term trends. However, in 2000, the number of severely disabled children was reported to be consistently more than double for boys than for girls of the same age group (ESRC 2006). The Department of Works and Pensions (DWP 2006) estimated that there were over 700,000 disabled children in the UK, which equates to around 1 in 20 children. This contrasts with Emerson and Hatton's (2005) estimation that in Britain there were approximately 1.2 million children under 17 who could be considered 'at risk' of disability. This clearly reflects differrng approaches in defining disability. Nevertheless it is clear that a substantial number of children have some form of disability, and consequently the position of the child, siblings and families should be assessed to provide a better understanding of their needs.

It is evident that children with disabilities have individual needs, reflected in the Children Act 1989 (s17(10)(c)). Their lives will not be the same as those of their peers, and even if disability were not an issue, the sense of having an impairment makes a difference which separates their experiences from those of others. Clearly, their needs and those of their families should be identified and met by providing the necessary services; and if it is not possible to identify the child's view of his or her needs, then that of the nearest family member, usually a parent (often the mother), should be sought.

Professional workers are also required to identify what family members say *they* need to help themselves, and to gather their reflections on what is useful, along with professional views, observation and consideration of such needs – and from these findings formulate what should be the professional response. This is basic to the ASPIRE model with its stages of ASsessment, Planning, Interventions, and Review and Evaluation which acts as a guide to the staging process of meeting needs (Burke and Cigno 2000, p.9; Sutton 1994, p.26). However, it should be clear that presenting a set of initials for a methodological assessment does little to introduce the sense of understanding that human need commands; it cannot and does not reflect on the quality or accuracy of an assessment or its evaluation. Following *Every Child Matters* (2006), reviews and recommendations for practice introduced the Common Assessment Framework (CAF) which is designed to:

> help practitioners assess children's additional needs for services earlier and more effectively, develop a common understanding of those needs and agree a process for working together to meet those needs. (DfES 2006a, p.2)

Importantly, the CAF requires work with other agencies, while indicating the need for a lead professional – which should help to unify practice when undertaking an assessment of child needs. Disability, in terms of child needs, in such an assessment would link with areas covering a range of developmental consequences, particularly concerning general health, physical development, speech and language, and social and emotional development. However, while this comprehensive review of child needs may seem laudable, putting disability into the picture may seemingly be more indicative of the child's limitations and impairment as complex needs, rather than being indicative of environmental restrictions and exclusions despite a mention of social and community resources (DfES 2006a, p.32).

Such tools are merely that: they introduce a sequencing of events, which may be transcended by crisis, or critical events, with professional judgement being exercised to determine whether a process is followed or is not appropriate in a given situation. The danger is that students on practice experience, and those in the early stages of their professional careers, may believe that a procedure represents some form of conceptual understanding of need, when it is little more than a means to systematise a record of chronological events, listing details which may then appear to have been understood. ASPIRE and assessment frameworks provide systematic tools; they have utility, and facilitate information flow between professionals. However, they do not represent professional judgement, or indeed any sense of scale concerning social problems, and consequently they are of limited value in understanding the consequences of a disabling impairment on the child and family. A brief look at the needs of a child helps to illustrate this critique.

The child

In the context of assessment, the needs of a disabled child should not be solely governed by medical descriptions. As children first, their needs will in many ways be common with other children, and in other ways will be unique. Research may tend to exclude the voice of the child (hence my focus on special needs and siblings of disabled children throughout this text) in concentrating on the needs of the family; see Clarke (2006, p.43) citing Shakespeare et al. (1999). Clarke indicates that a disabled child may be marginalised because of the tension between differing needs in the family, such that the rights of the disabled child are excluded and need identification and representation. Consequently, in any discussion that centres on the child, whether disability is an issue or not, at least two concepts apply which may be represented on the dimensions of (1) power and powerlessness and (2) social inclusion and exclusion. In responding to and recognising that a child is, to some extents, powerless and may experience exclusion, then the professionals involved need to make a clear demarcation about whose needs are being met: the child's, the carers', or those of other family members (Burke and Cigno 2000, p.4).

Locus of control

The concept of powerlessness requires a professional evaluation, as does the need for inclusion. A related concept, which helps evaluate whether someone is powerful or powerless, is the locus of control which was identified by Lefcourt (1976) and Burke (1998, 2004). Essentially, control is viewed as either internal or external. Individuals who take responsibility for their own actions have an internal locus of control. In other words, they take control of situations that impact on their lives and make their own decisions. Those who depend on others to make decisions for them are people who are subject to the control of others; they have an external locus of control. The sense of internal or external control is useful in the following case examination.

The case of Ashley X

The case of Ashley X of Los Angeles, as reported by Ayres (2007), is worthy of note here. Afflicted with a severe brain impairment known as static encephalopathy, Ashley cannot walk, talk, keep her head up in bed or even swallow food. Her parents argued that 'keeping her small' was the best way to improve the quality of her life, not to make life more convenient for them.

In this case, Ashley's parents agreed with medical advice, when she was six years old, to remove her uterus, among other procedures designed to stunt her growth so that she would remain the size of a child for the rest of her life. The issue of whose interests were being served should be considered. It may be thought that the carers are being served, despite the assertion that this was not the case, because Ashley's needs were subjugated to those of her parents. Her parents sought medical advice and also received further advice from an ethical committee that considered the need for surgical intervention. All agreed that the procedure would be of benefit to both child and carers and allowed the procedure to occur.

Comment

It might be helpful to speculate as to whether the procedure would have been agreed within the UK. Under the Children Act 1989, the 'child's welfare' is a paramount consideration (s1(1)), and the wishes and feelings of the child should be ascertained (s1(3)). It is probable that, in the UK, surgery that is not required on health grounds would not be viewed as necessarily in line with the welfare needs of the child. Indeed, it is arguable that from the requirement to identify a child's needs it is necessary to maintain a child's standard of health or development (s17(10)(a)) and emphasis would be given to the child's right to reasonable development physically and not to restrict it such that his or her health or development would be likely to be significantly impaired (s17(10)(b)). Further, a disabled child is considered to be a child in need (s17(10)(c)), or in other words the local authority has a duty to meet those needs. In the UK, therefore, it is arguable that the surgery on Ashley might not be considered legal if her needs were considered to be infringed.

These issues are difficult to comprehend without the full details of this case, with parents who are well-meaning; but it might be considered a matter of disability rights that an operative procedure that is not required on health grounds amounts to an abuse of power on a vulnerable individual. This is because the medical procedures could be considered to cause the child to suffer significant harm (s44).

The question then arises as to the advice Ashley's parents received. It is arguable that this type of example shows the power of the medical model to influence parental decisions away from the child's needs toward a medical resolution of the child's *management problems*. It is useful then to employ the concept concerning the locus of control. All one has to do is to try to understand the parents' situation, a situation where they are desperately trying to do the best for their child after six years of caring for her. In asking for help, some transfer of power takes place. What should they do? They are under stress. Medical advice is that there is a longer-term solution and that is sanctioned by the ethics committee, but is the committee view correct? Parents making decisions under duress, as even a summary consideration of crisis intervention theory will tell us (Katz 1975; Rapoport 1970), will tend to go along with a recommended course. The locus of control is no longer with the parents.

Clearly, social and medically based decisions do suggest differing courses in a case of this type. The medical model would stress that the procedure recognised Ashley's situation as a severely disabled child whose best interests were served, in a medical solution to her needs, by maintaining her child-like status. The social model of disability would indicate that the child is effectively victimised by the medical profession which, in carrying out the surgery, rendered Ashley as infant-like in size, sterilised, such that her sexuality, and any sensations related to it, are permanently denied.

Parental protectiveness of children with disabilities

According to Craft and Brown (1994), an individual with learning or significant communication difficulties may be susceptible to the undesired influences of others and may need some form of protection and support. Consequently parents of children with these difficulties may become over-protective, and so minimise opportunities for their child. The effect of over-protection is usually to reduce risk, as the parent sees the child's vulnerability to undesirable influences. The need is to determine what risks are acceptable against those that are not, and there should be a balance between the two.

Risk may be quantified as an 'agency measure of concern' and thus indicate a responsibility to the user. This combines a professional workplace and client-based approach. Agency workers who fail to detect or recognise risk may themselves be viewed as putting users at a higher risk than is acceptable due to their inaction or a lack of recognition of critical events (Burke 1999). Training to overcome such negative interventions is clearly necessary. Assessment in practice needs an integrated model, a social process model to complement the medical.

It may, nevertheless, take an outside influence to enable parents to appreciate whether they are being over-protective, in denying opportunities for their child or promoting procedures that may be considered harmful (as in the Ashley X case). In the ASPIRE model, practice may build on such conceptual understandings, with competing needs, that require the professional application of knowledge but which identify and locate the sense of powerlessness or exclusion experienced by the child before making life-changing recommendations.

The pursuit of knowledge includes the need to understand the need for support, the systems of help and self-help, which may be applicable, combined with an understanding of how to prevent situations from becoming more difficult. These reflections are based on a social perspective, as indicated by the social model of disability, and are intended to aid our understanding of family functioning. Thus, the intention here is to recognise the difficulties faced by family members and in particular to improve our understanding of the needs of the disabled child. Practice consequently may have a shifting focus and inevitably some element of competing needs will emerge. Professionalism is about assessing these needs and indicating which is the most urgent while recognising that all require some degree of attention.

Practice implications

A basic tenet of social work involves matching available services to assessed need. The NHS and Community Care Act 1990 reflects this view by outlining the main duty of assessment in meeting the needs of individuals for services (s47). The issue arises, nevertheless, about the way the assessment process works, especially if an assessment indicates a need for a service that does not exist. The duty on the professional worker is to obtain a service for which resources may not exist, or are in scant supply, due to the assessment made by the professional. On the other hand, a professional assessment carries the implication that, in determining need, the professional is treating the disabled child and family as dependent on the professional's opinion rather than necessarily contributing to a joint decision no matter how conciliatory the meetings between the parties involved. This is because the social model of disability is about a social construction between the service user and family that may inadvertently reinforce the idea of 'disability' as 'dependent' rather than asserting the rights of individuals and families. Thompson (2001, p.116) considers that such a view is indicative of a form of 'social oppression' because disability is being equated with dependency and 'non-contribution to mainstream society'.

In order to improve service provision there is a necessary step to improve agency collaboration. Multi-agency collaboration may be promoted by:

- agencies working under one roof to enable professionals to liaise informally

- encouraging parental empowerment and partnership so that parents and their child can access agency resources quickly, because decisions are enabled by the proximity of professional staff (Burke and Cigno 2000, p.134).

However, it is not always clear whether one professional has sanction over another, and consequently professional autonomy and responsibility may be compromised if one profession is expected to fall in line with another. For example, consultants might decide to hold a pre-meeting to determine a preferred course that is then presented to social care professionals and, more importantly, to the family involved. If police action (as may occur in a suspected child protection case) is determined independently of conference activity, the sense of working together is also lost. This is a difficult call, to determine the respective inputs of professionals when enabling family functioning by providing resources for a disabled child. This situation may improve with the Common Assessment Framework (DfES 2006a, p.2) when a lead professional is identified and responsible for coordinating actions to be taken, although professional differences will always remain to be resolved.

It is clear that rules of practice might generate dependency, and lead to difficulty for families to articulate their own needs when the aim should be to promote independent living and social inclusion. Unfortunately, it is not easy for mainstream professional practitioners to escape typified reactions no matter how conscientious they may be. It is an issue where training lags behind research-engendered understanding of user experiences, such that 'good practice' is constantly refined as our understanding improves.

Practice notes

What is the difference between disability and impairment?
Central to the discussion on working with families and children with disabilities is the view that an impairment represents an individual condition which may be intellectual, physical or a loss following an accident. This is different from disability as a social construct, a consequence of negative attitudes or physical barriers that disadvantage people considered to be disabled.

How does the social model of disability make a difference?
This model is intended to show how disabilities are generated beyond an impairment, due to a reaction to disabled people that discriminates against them through barriers to access and attitudinal reactions of a negative type. Society can reduce a sense of disability by accepting people with impairments, by improving access for those with mobility problems, by not being afraid of disability, and by promoting inclusive policies and practices toward people with disabilities.

What about the medical model of disability – surely that is important to maintain?
The problem with the medical world is that people tend to be treated according to their illness, so the patient becomes, for example, the 'heart patient', and some sense of the individuality of the person is lost in the process. With a 'disabled person' the nature of the condition may take

precedence over the individual, so disabled people may be encouraged to undergo treatments that they might otherwise not consider necessary.

Why consider the 'locus of control'?
An internal locus is when decisions are taken by the individual; an external control exists when other people take those decisions. This simple distinction helps evaluate whether individuals make choices within their lives or if they expect others to do so on their behalf. It is a useful way of recognising the influences in someone's life and helps to identify the elements of control that exist. Understanding the direction of controlling influences enables those individuals to realise the reality of their situation, and with professional support, where needed, will enable a degree of understanding and redirection within their lives.

Will the Common Assessment Framework (CAF) make a difference?
Any moves to improve practice must be welcomed, especially when this involves identifying a lead professional responsible for coordinating action plans based on fuller and more clearly detailed assessment procedures. But procedures alone will not and cannot substitute for professional decision-making when a judgement on action has to be made; even if better informed by the guidance provided, procedures alone cannot substitute for the decision itself. Further, procedures cannot require all professions to work to the same code of practice; and, although encouraging interprofessional working and planning, some elements of pre-planning may remain especially when professionals firmly disagree on the desired outcome to be achieved. More fundamentally, the question of how the family with a disabled child fits into a generalised assessment framework has also to be addressed, given that a better specialised understanding of 'child needs' is required in this area. A difference will be made by the CAF, but whether or not it makes a sufficient difference for children with disabilities and their families remains to be seen.

Do we need to make a distinction between parents and carers?
Yes, parents are usually the carers of their offspring, but substitute parenting can be provided by foster carers who are not necessarily related to the family. So parents are normally biologically related to those being cared for, as birth parents, while substitute carers are not so directly

related. But parents are only carers if actively looking after their child, and anyone who looks after members of a family, whose needs have to be met, fulfils this role. Parents who do not care for their child are clearly not carers. Essentially it is the biological relationship that makes the distinction between parents (which cannot be altered) and carers. Caring depends on the activity of the hands-on relationship and that clarifies who is the carer. In Chapter 6, the role of *young carers* is considered within the family relationship, where siblings take direct responsibility for the care of a disabled brother or sister (or sometimes a disabled parent), rather than the more usual arrangement of parents caring for their children.

Chapter 2

Stigma, Need and Service Provision

Disability, when it affects the child, is a family matter, although disability itself is not something that is necessarily understood in terms of its consequences for the family. In this chapter, the intent is to examine stigma and the service provision for families with disabled children, as medically and socially defined. The impact of a child's disability is, it will be shown, not just about the child, it becomes part of the family's identity. This identity with disability is partly configured by social relationships which tend to reinforce an understanding of disability as a traumatic experience. Further, this chapter considers the legal duty to assist the disabled child and members of the child's family.

The social aspect of disability is clarified by reference to stigma as defined by Goffman (1963), who suggests that some groups of people are not treated the same as others and will exist on the margins of society. Such experiences lead these individuals to have a devalued status, and in Goffman's accounts were represented by those who were labelled 'mentally ill'. However, other stigmatised groups may include those with minority group membership, and of course, those who have certain types of disabilities. Stigma carries the sense of not being true to culturally desired norms of behaviour, and consequently such individuals have what Goffman calls a 'spoiled identity'. Goffman's views are important in gaining a sense of how social events make a difference to disability; but when combined with a consideration of the medical and social model of disability, they extend our understanding of the process that transforms an impairment into a 'disabled identity'.

Stigmatisation
Stigmatisation is a process that can be identified within families with disabled children when social interactions promote a sense of individual

disadvantage. Social disadvantage itself, as indicated by Graham and Power (2004), is a concept which indicates that we do not all have the same opportunities and fortune because our social systems favour some over others. Abercrombie, Hill and Turner (2000) reveal that the infra-structure of social systems fails certain groups and communities, such that an individual allocation of blame is, at best, erroneous, because it is more probable that the wider elements of social structure and policy implementation are the source of the problem.

Indeed, Scott, Campbell and Brown (2002) suggest that families perceived as 'high risk' are not inherently different from others in disad-vantaged circumstances. This seems to indicate that stigma is a means for blame and discrimination based on perceptual differentiation rather than actual or physical difference: its construction identified by location, grouping or specific situations. A causal explanation might suggest, however, that individuals within any given social system are necessarily linked in some way, that individual difficulties are invariably connected with the social fabric that builds families, communities and, ultimately, centres for urban growth or decline.

Whatever the nature of social systems that exist, it is implicit that any failure to recognise difference, as with disability, as a positive attribute will conversely allow or promote negativity as its root causation. This helps to establish a 'spoilt identity' for those that seem different. If an interaction is not understood, it is perhaps easier to ignore rather than to challenge its foundation. This conception of individuals within the social system, who practise avoidance but, faced with uncertainty, admonish blame, fits with the circumstances of families who experience normality themselves but feel oppressed and discriminated against. This fit is suggestive of an associative model, with the 'spoilt identity' of dis-ability reflecting uncertainty and disadvantage by a generalised other.

Stigma, according to Goffman (1963), concerns an individual trait that has an undesirable social impact such that, in potential social exchanges, the identification of that difference often results in negative reactions. This may be illustrated by reference to Scott (1969) who, in a discussion on the impact of 'blindness', suggested that stigma is the reaction felt by 'normal' individuals in discrediting people who are blind and hence different, such that a person who is blind has a 'spoilt iden-tity', a term previously used by Goffman to indicate a negative reaction. The consequence may result in avoidance by particular groups of indi-viduals who are perceived as different. This construction of difference would indicate that a potential disadvantage exists for the minority because the experience of stigmatisation puts individuals into categories or groupings that reduce social expectations and achievement, and rather than making the lives of those subject to such experiences socially and emotionally content it tends to reinforce negative stereotypical reactions.

In moving this discussion forward, it is helpful to examine stigma in relation to childhood disabilities. Stigma, as described by Burke (2007), can be identified in three ways:

- stigma concerning social exchanges in day-to-day interactions
- stigma of a situational type – the effect of location and place
- stigma that has structural associations – how people are treated by professionals and officials.

These forms of stigma are examined in more detail below.

Social stigma

Goffman (1963) suggests that no groups of people are treated the same and this leads some individuals to have a devalued status. Goffman (1974, p.56) later described disabling conditions as stigmatising because of interactions between individuals when one does not meet the expectations of the other. Social stigma in relation to childhood disability occurs, therefore, where the child has what Goffman referred to as a 'spoiled identity'. This occurs when an interaction is preventing an acceptance, an engagement or any real opportunity for communication with others because the perceived disabled child is found by others to be unacceptable. People who experience negative social reactions to themselves do not correspond to the 'norm' and they experience a feeling of social stigmatisation; they are simply made to feel that they do not belong.

Situational stigma

Situational stigma is akin to disqualification before any attempt to interact or to belong, due to some disadvantage, quality or experience that is not accepted by others in a position of judgement. Situational elements of stigma may arise when membership of a group is questioned. For example, Barnes and Mercer (2003, p.9), in their discussion of the divide between 'able-bodied and disabled people', explain that being disabled is viewed, at best, as 'unfortunate' by the non-disabled group, which is akin to being perceived as being unworthy, or is essentially an explicit non-acceptance and rejection of disability in any manifestation without even considering the individual. Consequently, the 'normal' group does not consider feasible any form of engagement between the accepted and non-accepted individuals; this is exclusion of those deemed not fit to match the main reference criteria, like not being allowed to join a club for some spurious reason. Indeed, situational stigma is a form of pre-judged social exclusion and discrimination, such that social contact is avoided at all costs and is effectively impossible.

Structural stigma

The third type of stigma is structural, when, for example, the diagnosis of an impairment may exclude opportunities otherwise available to the non-impaired. Gillman (2004, p.253) cites the diagnosis of 'learning difficulty' that serves to promote 'prejudicial and discriminatory attitudes in some professionals, which may lead to disrespectful or dehumanising treatment of individuals who are seeking support'. She goes on to suggest that, once such a diagnosis is made, further conditions are sought to provide a resulting 'dual diagnosis'. In a sense, the seeking of additional conditions is associative, in the belief that somehow one is a contagion of the other. However, the reality is that disabled people feel blamed and ridiculed for their disability (Morris 1996): the need is to challenge such views.

Comment

It is evident that disability (as a social construction) has become identified as a personal problem or condition that should be overcome on an individual basis; in turn, this leads to social exclusion. The experiences of childhood disability belong to the family as each member shares the experience of the other to some degree. In a perfect situation, where exclusion and neglect does not occur, then this model of disability would cease to exist because it would not help our understanding of the experience faced by the 'disabled family' as a unit. Indeed, Thompson's (2001) model of anti-discriminatory practice is about changing individual, situational and cultural attitudes; these might equally apply to the social model of disability.

The impact of stigmatising situations is experienced by individuals who are perceived as different through the process of social, situational and structural factors as mentioned above, but the question of how stigma becomes an associative state for others who are close to such individuals, whether family members or professionals working with the family, needs further examination.

Stigma and disability by association

Stigma by association was discussed by Östman and Kjellin (2002). In relation to the impact on the families who lived with individuals who were diagnosed with a form of mental health illness, they reported that the concept had received comparatively little attention from empirical researchers. Further:

> Stigma affects not only people with mental illnesses, but their families as well. The process by which a person is stigmatised by virtue of association with another stigmatised individual...[is] 'associative' stigma. (p.494)

It is apparently the case that being a member of a family when one member is mentally ill places on the family an associative identity as though the family as a unit is 'mentally ill'. The resulting perceptions create a stigma that affects the social and wider familial activities, almost creating a fear of contagion in others beyond the immediate family unit.

Associative stigma is clearly not linked only to people with mental illness but is evident in a range of other situations where an individual is labelled with a 'problem'. Such 'problems' of association may be identified with HIV/AIDS, drug use, gender preference, or being 'looked after', as a child by a statutory body (see also Burke and Parker 2007). Labels themselves, although having the potential to stereotype in a negative sense, nevertheless serve to identify difference – as clarified by Lewis (1995). Difference, as with disability, should be accepted and included within the diversity of experience.

Disability by association may be identified in social interaction that causes an individual to feel stigmatised because he or she lives in a family with a disabled child. The concept of disability by association reflects the experience of siblings of disabled children (Burke 2004). Disability by association extends the social model of disability by demonstrating that the identity of disability is not entirely in the possession of disabled people themselves. It is recognised that disability has the potential to socially exclude a disabled person from social experiences (as with the issue of spoilt identity in stigmatisation) and consequently, as with mental illness, the family and siblings of the disabled individual experience an impact akin to that of the person with the disability.

The creation of a stigmatised other is initiated through an associative order and influences those closest to the individual, including siblings, family and relatives, and indeed workers in direct contact with the originating source: it is like a ripple of associative disadvantage (see Figure 2.1).

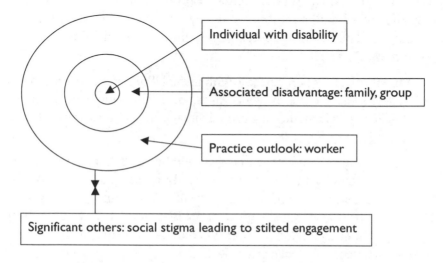

Figure 2.1 Circle of influence: stigma, associative disadvantage and practice relationships

Figure 2.1 indicates that the association of disadvantage is sufficient to cause a degree of stress in interactive exchanges. Consequently, the individual, the family, even the professional worker with the family, might be viewed by significant others with some uncertainty. Significant others – people who influence our lives – as identified by Fawcett (2000), may be understood by reference to Foucault's pragmatic conceptualisation of resistance in power relationships: 'There are no relationships without resistance' (Foucault 1980, p.142). Stigmatisation may be a reflection that defines the power relationship, when the nature of interactions tests an acceptance or otherwise, and where the stigmatised individual may be expected to show some form of resistance to being placed within a particular category or grouping. Disability by association typifies the potential resistance in power relationships, and may result in the avoidance of an identity with disability, or create a conflict of interests in gaining acceptance for the presence of disability.

Family and child disability services as part of a legal requirement

The legal requirement for service provision for families and children is germane to the Children Act 1989. Section 17(1)(a)(b) states that a duty exists (on the local authority) to safeguard and promote the upbringing of children by their families. A child with a disability is considered to be 'in need' within the meaning of the Act (s17(10)(c)). In determining the nature of 'the family', in providing for a 'child in need', then s17(10) of the Act defines the family as consisting of 'any person who has parental responsibilities for the child and *any other person with whom he has been living*' (my emphasis). Indeed, the Department of Health (2000a, p.9) indicates that 'services may be provided to any member of the family in order to assist a child in need' (s17(3) of the Children Act 1989). Assessing the needs of the family, including siblings, as carers themselves, is recognised within the Carer (Recognition and Services) Act 1995. Professionals working with the families of children with disabilities would fit within this legal framework where the requirement is to consider all family members within the assessment process.

In October 2000, the Human Rights Act 1998 was implemented; it is not specifically related to children, but its impact is likely to be significant. This is true despite the fact that the Children Act 1989 and the Family Law Act 1996 were drafted, according to Cleave (2000), to be compatible with the Convention for the Protection of Human Rights and Fundamental Freedoms, a convention incorporated within the Human Rights Act 1998. In particular, the Act reinforced the right of the individual to be free of discrimination, is respecting of family life and privacy, and introduced concepts concerning gender, ethnic groups and people with disabilities. The right to a private family life is fundamental, a concept which incorporates all family members. Yet, as Cleave suggests, if local authorities follow the *Children Act Best Practice Guidance*, the Act would make little statutory difference. However, the application of the Act will arise in situations when arbitrary acts by the state intrude on the right to private life, where each family member has equal rights.

The question of legal responsibilities and the need to reflect on and consider the views of young people is central to government policy, and specifically was commented on by Jacqui Smith (2002), then Minister of

State for Health, in a letter on the Department of Health Action Plan, indicating that the plan:

> shows how serious we are about listening to the views of children and young people and the steps we are taking to extent this work across the entire Department. (Letter dated 20 June 2002)

The intent was to develop a policy within the modernising social services agenda that is designed to improve services for children. Indeed, the agenda for Modernising Social Services (DoH 1998) stated that:

> Standards of delivery and achievements are unreliable, and although many children benefit from social services, too many are let down. (Quote in para. 3.2)

These issues are central to child care practices, but the fear here is that families with disabled children may continue to be sidelined. The continued government concern, which set up the Social Exclusion Unit and produced reports like *Valuing People* (DoH 2001b), points toward providing services in line with what people want, working in partnership and promoting 'rights, responsibilities, citizenship and participation' (DoH 2001b, p.37). All this indicates that individuals *should* be able to express their needs and that professionals should respond to them in the most appropriate way. Yet, in my research, the need is to provide support for families within the scope of the existing legislation, and the evidence provided in the following chapters demonstrates how service provision does not always meet the needs of the family, parents, siblings and the child with a disability. It is evident that families continue to remain vulnerable, unsupported and isolated. Resources provision for families, as well as for disabled children themselves, is of vital consideration when assessing family needs.

Understanding special educational needs

The United Nations Convention reminds us that children have the right to an opinion based on information they have received, and that such opinion should be considered according to their age, maturity and capabilities (United Nations Convention 1989, articles 12 and 13). With regard to the education of children with disabilities, Barnes and Mercer (2003, p.45) express the view that the system should include 'competition choice and selection'. Seeking their views is central to understanding the wishes and feelings of young people, and forms part of the underpinning of the Children Act 1989. This Act promotes child decision-making rights within a framework that balances the dual interests of parents with responsibility for their child with the views of the child, taking the child's view seriously (Fortin 2003, p.9). The need for an independent voice for the child should be promoted (Burke and Montgomery 2003): it is part of the child's right to be heard; it is fundamental to the child's right to be treated as an independent player, and is recognised within the Human Rights Act 1998 (Fortin 2003, p.59).

When educational professionals take decisions concerning the future welfare of the child then the Children Act 1989 requires that the child's view should be included; need is clarified within this Act as being an identifier due to disability (s17(10)(c)). The Special Educational Needs and Disability Act 2001 now makes it unlawful for institutions to treat a disabled person 'less favourably' than non-disabled people, so the 'disabled' child's right to mainstream education is now established in law. However, the Mental Health Act 1983 refers to 'mental handicap' and 'mental impairment' to compound the sense of learning disability and special needs as an amorphous group whose identity is less clear. The range of seemingly contradictory terminology has the propensity to undermine the voice and decision-making capacity of children and, in doing so, disempower them. Over a life course, learning that his or her view does count would establish an important principle for the child in seeking personal life wishes in the years to come.

It is perhaps fortunate that the publication *Valuing People* (DoH 2001b) argues for choice and opportunity for people with learning disabilities, and Fyson and Simons (2003) agree that this need is achievable by promoting positive change – although it is recognised that *Valuing People* does not target children in the same way as adults. In policy terms, the active involvement of young people in the provision of services is, however, established by the Department of Health in expressing the need for assessment (2004a, p.5). Choice is central to the planning process that influences people's lives, and more than a single option needs to be available if a positive choice is to be realised: this is a continuing point which surfaces in the promotion of a person-centred approach to planning and support (DoH 2004b, p.41).

The need for an ethical understanding
Although attention is drawn to the current legislation in Britain, the ethics governing professional practice is underpinned by the UN's

Convention on the Rights of the Child (United Nations 1989), which requires that *all children* should have the right to non-discrimination (article 2) and freedom of expression (article 12). When these rights are balanced with the child's right to dignity, the promotion of self-reliance and the facility to participate in the community (article 23), they represent the beginnings of an entitlement framework. In addition, all children should have the right to an education designed to encourage their fullest potential (articles 28, 29): any factors that deny these entitlements need to be documented and understood so that something may be done to remedy the situation.

The studies reported in this book are concerned with family experience and particularly that of children with special needs and the siblings of children with disabilities. Siblings may experience discrimination at school or in the neighbourhood, if not at home, due to their living in a family with a disabled child. This clearly shows that these experiences need to be understood, whether this is due to difference, disability or discrimination for whatever reason.

Fundamental to such a view are three concepts which link with those identified by Burke and Cigno (2000): inclusion, empowerment and neglect. Other frameworks identified in the White Paper *Valuing People* (DoH 2001b) concern learning disabled people's access to rights, independence, choice and inclusion; alternatively, another framework is suggested in *A Quality Strategy for Social Care* (DoH 2000b) which has a focus on rights, responsibilities, citizenship and participation. Whatever the choice for analysis, the intent is to focus on areas of need that might be subject to abuse or neglect. Essentially this requires a balanced understanding of the needs of parents and of their disabled children, including recognition of the needs of siblings.

Inclusive practice: an example from special education

Inclusive practice can simply mean involving the 'service user' in any plans that are initiated to resolve difficulties and problems. However, inclusion for children with disabilities concerns access to entitlements within a framework of service provision and user protection for vulnerable groups. Obtaining entitlements may be assisted via practice initiatives and sharing the knowledge base of services that are available. The need for an ethical understanding when services are provided might question the sense that one law applies to the poor and another to the rich. For example, Ruth Kelly, a Cabinet member and former minister for education, secured a place for her son who had learning difficulties at a privately run school, and was criticised for placing the government under acute pressure. The local authority is obliged to fund places for children with special needs, and her son received an advantage not available to less well off families (BBC News 2007a).

It might then be suggested that the local authority places were inferior, so a family dependent on the local authority service would receive a second-rate service, as these children are excluded from selective education on the grounds of income. The politics of this are not debated here; the issue is of a two-level service, because if inclusion is to work, a child with special needs should have equal access to all available and suitable educational services. It is interesting to note, however, that the European Development Fund (2002) addresses the issue of selective education:

> Notwithstanding the best intentions, it is conceded that all too often the result [of special programmes, specialised institutions, special educators] has been exclusion; differentiation becoming a form of discrimination, leaving children with special needs outside the mainstream of school life and later, as adults, outside community social and cultural life in general. (pp.63–64)

This suggests that special education itself is a form of exclusion, because of the selective policies in operation. Nevertheless most parents interviewed within my research would consider that it is their right to choose from the best available educational resources available, whether in special or mainstream education. The issues of special education and mainstream provision are discussed further in Chapter 5.

Social inclusion, in relation to professional practice, emphasises the need to avail individuals of services in a positive way to ensure that needs are met. Oliver and Barnes (1998, p.49) consider the shift to community-based services as being a professionally determined, needs-based model, which is essentially exclusive in its ability to segregate and target services. Professionals are therefore in danger of not providing services across the board to those needing them. In the first place, however, those who work with families need to recognise that disability makes a difference to families, that difference permeates all family members, and that an inequality of service provision may be detrimental to the wellbeing of the child. Through segregation in service provision, disabilities and their consequences for the child impact on family members too.

Ethnicity: double oppression

In their report on minority ethnic families, Chamba *et al.* (1999) demonstrated the greater disadvantage facing minority groups comparing white families with Indian and Black/Caribbean families. They reported that minority groups had the least support from their extended families owing to families not living in their locality. The degree of unmet needs was higher than found in white families, indicating that ethnic families with severely disabled children were very poorly served by social care agencies. Phillips (1998) indicated that families with disabled children who were from ethnic groups suffered a double disadvantage, due to the impact of childhood disability and ethnicity. This is precisely the situation reported by Burke (2004, p.56) concerning the case of Rani and Ahmed, children of a family who experienced segregation within a small village owing to childhood disability and non-acceptance in the local community due to their ethnic background. Clearly, discrimination operates at both levels, with ethnic difference and disability being barriers to acceptance for ethnic groups within the wider population.

A balance of services

It is apparent that enabling choices to be made is vital to the needs of individuals, especially so if an element of choice is lacking for some family members owing to low expectations and a lack of energy to become empowered. This is the experience of learned helplessness, where failure in terms of achieving desired outcomes is viewed as unattainable (Balter and Tamis-LeMonda 2003). Learned helplessness creates a sense of internalised failure, and professional advisors who struggle to find adequate resources to meet needs perpetuate this sense of dependency.

In trying to achieve a better balance of service provision, Howard (1999) states:

> The key test of the effectiveness of a modern council will be the extent to which it delivers 'local services to local people'. To do this, equalities issues should be built in from the start, which will involve devising appropriate consultation mechanisms. (p.28)

In other words, services should be provided within the locality based on need and services, and should not discriminate based on ethnicity. Asking people what they want and providing the necessary services should be a straightforward entitlement – in some ways reflecting consumer opinion, in providing the services asked for by families with disabled children.

These experiences were implicitly identified in a pilot study by Burke and Montgomery (2000), and now, following that research, it is possible to clarify what might be considered a 'rights framework'. This is compatible with government policy and practice-related recommendations within Department of Health reports on *A Quality Strategy for Social Care* (2000b), *Valuing People* (2001b) and *Planning with People* (2001a, 2002) which engender an inclusive approach to working with families and with professionals. This understanding begins to prescribe a role for welfare professionals when enabling families to become included families, by helping them to make choices from a range of support services.

It certainly appears to be the case, as demonstrated by Burke and Cigno (1996), that most families welcome the offer of professional support, which I can now confirm following four research studies as outlined in the Appendix. It is apparent, too, that siblings of disabled children also need to be included in discussions with parents and professional representatives, but they are too easily excluded when they could contribute to decisions and identify their need for services. Services are considered a basic entitlement for the family, and ensuring services are delivered is part of positive practice that needs more than just an encouraging push.

Practice notes

Is stigma and the sense of a 'spoiled identity' really applicable to professional work?

One mechanism which discriminates against someone in a wheelchair is not to address the wheelchair user. This is stigmatising in the sense that a judgement is made that equates physical incapacity with intellectual inability. Similarly a 'spoiled identity' is the stereotyping of certain individuals because of a perceived impairment, and consequently excluding those individuals from social opportunities. Understanding these concepts helps to identify whether individuals are treated equally or not, and hopefully will encourage the professional to redress the balance and encourage the acceptance of previously negatively labelled individuals.

What is disability by association?

This is about the fact that some people are discriminated against because of perceived differences in their family relationships (i.e. a family with a child that has a disability) and this discrimination is applied to those associated with them. Indeed this applies not only to family members but also to professionals who work with the family. It is a reflection of the social model of disability where society constructs a disabled identity for the individual with an impairment and that social construction becomes identified with all those associated with the disabled person. It is like a fear that disability is communicable, it can somehow transfer from one to another like an invisible force, and therefore results in oppressive views unrepresentative of the actual nature of those individuals who are cast in a false light.

What is social stigma?

This is the element of an interactive experience when one discriminates against another because the other does not conform to group expectations. People who look or act differently from others are not accepted by the wider groups because of the perceived differences.

How is situational stigma experienced?

This is being judged unfavourably due to belonging to a different class, group or area. An example would be of being viewed as troublesome because of where you live; for example this might result in a comment of the type 'not from that estate!'

Is structural stigma any different from social and situational?

Yes. It occurs when people in authority treat other people as not deserving owing to a view that 'these people' are somehow inferior. This may occur in a job interview where the interviewer is in judgement over the interviewee; it will be informed by social and situational stigma although the authority of one over another is more direct. This could be the experience of a service user during an interview when the social worker makes an assessment based on personal beliefs rather than professional values. Anti-oppressive practices need to be reinforced to ensure that the user is not being unfairly treated.

What are ethics?

Ethics concern the application of values and the recognition that people have individual rights. Often this may be outlined in a code of practice or entitlements to be upheld by professional groups. Fundamental to an ethical understanding is the need to respect the rights of individuals. This should occur in a professional relationship, and includes maintaining the rights of users or carers to confidentiality, upholding their right to choice, difference or normality, protection and inclusion, and always, of ensuring fair treatment.

What do we mean by 'looked-after children' and 'service user'?

'Looked-after children' is the term used to refer to children within the care of the local authority, whether as a result of a legal requirement or due to an agreement with the child's carers. Caring is provided by foster parents, in residential care or with extended family members. When looked-after children are cared for in this way they are utilising local authority services. The term 'service user' will apply to any individual or family being offered a service by the local authority.

Chapter 3

The Impact of Childhood Disability: The Family Experience

This chapter presents the family experience of childhood disability and reflects on both the literature and evidence initially gathered from the studies outlined in the Appendix. It is apparent that the birth of a disabled child requires a major change in the expectations of the family and, as with any new experience, it will produce an increased level of anxiety, stress and uncertainty, due in part to a fear of the unknown (Lazarus and Foulkman 1984). This chapter also illustrates childhood disability by utilising a number of representative quotations from the families involved in these studies.

Learning about a disabled child

According to Trute and Hiebert-Murphy (2002), the diagnosis of a childhood disability carries an emotional adjustment for the parents ranging from crisis reactions to positive acceptance. A major change of lifestyle has to be accomplished and may be anticipated when a child is born, whether first born or a later addition to the family. However, the initial diagnosis of childhood disability may impart additional stresses which have to be overcome, especially if parents do not understand the nature of the disability or its possible consequences for the child and the family's future. The latter gives rise to uncertainty, and the adjustment to living with a disabled child is partly attributed to the need to deal with change. Accordingly, it is interesting to examine data from my own research which questions the timing of the diagnosis of childhood disability, whether following the birth of a child or at a later stage. As a result of the initial concerns raised in my earlier study (Burke and Cigno 1996) a question was added to the main survey questionnaire in the second study, the siblings research, about the detection of a child's disability and the nature of the disability.

Discovering that a child in the family has a disability

The initial reaction to having a new baby in the family is usually one of celebration. A new child requires major family readjustments whether or not a disability has been diagnosed or is evident. It is probable that some parents will be informed, prior to birth, that the baby will be disabled. Over the past 20 years, the advent of antenatal testing has made it possible to detect a baby's future disability and raise the consideration of whether a pregnancy should continue. These are extremely difficult issues for the parents and some may feel pressured into making a termination decision that they might regret in years to come (Burke and Cigno 2000, pp.87–88). The diagnosis of disability is often a shock to parents and they are likely to experience a range of emotions, ranging from the delight of having a newborn child to anger, denial and grief reactions (Frude 1991; Knight 1996; Russell 1997). People do not all have stereotypical reactions and consequently needs will not be the same in all families or for all situations.

As the research progressed from the first to the second and third studies, my own knowledge of disability had increased (see Appendix, Figure A.1) and so questions were asked about the early diagnosis of childhood disability and its consequences. Discussions with an advisory group also made it clear that parents were very concerned about gaining a diagnosis and information about the future effects of disability on the family. This may seem an obvious point, but the shift in thinking involved required an identification and acceptance of disability as an immediate factor in someone's life, contrasted with the probability that once a medical diagnosis was confirmed the family had then to adjust to a lifelong association with disability. The transitional adjustment to acceptance seemed to centre on the point of understanding that a child, possibly your child, has a disability, and often that may coincide (but not necessarily so) with the diagnosis of a condition which may not previously have been heard of by the parents. The child's parents may suspect that a disability exists before confirmation is made by a medical practitioner, but once the diagnosis is confirmed it represents a pivotal point of no return and requires an adjustment by most parents, to accept the fact that their child is actually disabled (the term parents used rather than 'impairment').

In examining the data from studies two and three it became apparent that a large proportion of parents received the diagnosis of their child's disability before the age of one year (48% study three and 38% study four; see Figure 3.1), while the majority of children were diagnosed after the age of one year (respectively 52% and 62%). However, a considerable number of children were still awaiting a diagnosis beyond the age of five years, and although there was some variation in the two studies the trends are clear: most children are diagnosed before the age of two years, while a smaller but significant minority remain undiagnosed beyond the age of five years.

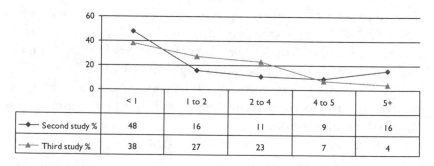

	< 1	1 to 2	2 to 4	4 to 5	5+
Second study %	48	16	11	9	16
Third study %	38	27	23	7	4

Figure 3.1 Age at diagnosis of disability

This raises the issue of why some children are diagnosed early and others later. In order to gain some understanding of these tendencies, reference to the nature of the disabilities identified is helpful, and these are shown in Figure 3.2.

It will be immediately apparent that both studies show a remarkable consistency for the groupings identified. This is a little surprising given that the groups were independent of each other, with the second study being locally based in the Hull region and the third corresponding mostly to North Lincolnshire. The former represents a full sample from a children's centre, the latter a random selection provided with access via a voluntary children's agency.

It is interesting to note that autism, with reference to the autistic spectrum, has the highest incidence of reportage by parents. It cannot be said that this reflects national trends, which comment on the increased prevalence of autistic spectrum (Wing and Potter 2002), or media

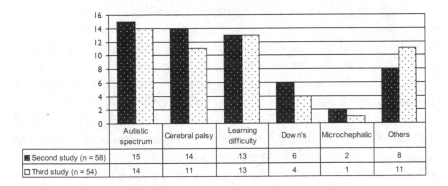

	Autistic spectrum	Cerebral palsy	Learning difficulty	Down's	Microchephalic	Others
■ Second study (n = 58)	15	14	13	6	2	8
□ Third study (n = 54)	14	11	13	4	1	11

Figure 3.2 Type of reported disability in child

reportage concerning speculation about the incidence as reported by BBC News (2007b) that autism is 'more common than thought'. This suggests, however – and the evidence in terms of prevalence supports the view – that the autistic spectrum was indicated as a first-mentioned disability across the studies reported for a significant group of children.

The data here provide an indication of apparently similar proportions of children within the autistic spectrum and within similar sized response populations. Learning disabilities, if including Down's syndrome children, is actually the highest group numerically, and so the research relating to siblings is more indicative of families where children with disabilities are predominantly representative of learning disabled. The question of whether autistic children are also learning disabled is not addressed (but see Shattock and Whiteley 2005), although if considered as a 'learning disability' then the type of disability would tend, from these results, to polarise into either learning disability or physical disability with some limited crossing-over between the two for certain types of disability.

The 'Others' category are conditions reported singly within both surveys which could not be represented with ease graphically because commonalities were not sufficiently evident for comparison purposes. Within the nineteen children (8 + 11) there were some with very rare conditions, including Batten's disease, Niemann–Pick disease, and other variously defined conditions ranging from challenging behaviour to epilepsy.

Sometimes children had multiple disabilities. Then the first-mentioned condition was used as the defining one for the research, although secondary disabilities might include epilepsy or other conditions, such that the results only gave an indication of the initially diagnosed disabilities and most parents and families were informed of this during the earlier stages of the child's development.

In over 60 per cent of all the cases reported in study two a medical consultant or GP confirmed the diagnosis. Interestingly, only 10 per cent of the sample knew, at birth, that their child had a disability, which corresponded with the ten children diagnosed with Down's syndrome.

It is clearly the case that knowing a child's disability at birth has a differing impact on the family to one diagnosed at the age of five: the children are at different stages developmentally and parental reactions will not be the same. Nevertheless, a label may not be the most important factor in sibling relationships. The sense of difference, reported in the pilot study (Burke and Montgomery 2000), 'Why can't she be like me?' (p.232), still persisted in some families and was a potential source of frustration and confusion between brothers and sisters with disabled siblings, especially when siblings got older and were more aware that their brother or sister was different. It is suggested that the needs of disabled children should be differentiated according to sex, and professionals should not be 'conceptualising disabled children as without gender' as reported by Middleton (1999, p.124). The percentage of disabled boys was higher in both studies (second study, 35:21; third study, 40:19), which equates to nearly 50 per cent more disabled boys than girls, a finding which is consistent with national estimates from the ESRC (2006).

Parental responses to a diagnosed condition

It is sometimes easier to repeat the words that parents used to show reactions to disability. This format will be followed to let the parents speak for themselves. Comments are selective although intended to be representative of others, as has been the aim with all four research studies cited within this text. The nature of certain conditions and impairments will have a variable impact on parents, but the resolution of some potential conflict for parents is represented by a view expressed on receiving a diagnosis confirming that the child is disabled: 'You know where you are, even if you are not sure where you are going.' (mother of seven-year-old Jamie, diagnosed with a learning disability). Another commented: 'We knew she was different, right from the start, but it helps when they [the medical profession] tell you what you know already (mother of 12-year-old Sandy, diagnosed with autistic tendencies).

Clearly it is important for parents to have a labelled condition because that helps with knowing where to turn for support as well as providing a realisation that possibly unresolved concerns may become identified with the condition, so comments like 'so that is why...' were not uncommon. The issue of a suspected condition becomes resolved with a diagnosis, which seemed centrally important to parents; and even when parental 'fears' were confirmed, the uncertainty about the nature of a condition would at least begin to be resolvable in the short term despite some considerable uncertainty about the future.

Stress

Stress may be defined in any number of ways, but for our purposes it is about uncertainties that are faced when our routines are changed or challenged. According to Atkinson *et al.* (1990), stress occurs when we are unsure of our ability to deal with the event that is perceived as threatening. A research study by Holmes and Rahe (Hopson 1981) suggests that stressful experiences may be cumulative to a point of intolerance by the individual: the greater the stressor, the greater the effort required to adapt. However, Hopson suggested that adjustments to stress are possible with a transitional sequence of adaptations that lead to an internalisation of the stressing experience once a full adjustment is achieved.

It is perfectly normal to experience an increase in stress when unexpected events are encountered, although Middleton (1999) argues that change can be a positive development. Living with a disabled child will increase the stress experienced by parents. Research by Baxter, Cummins and Yiolitis (2000) indicated that families with a disabled child experienced approximately double the stress of a family with a non-disabled child. So, dealing with disability is a major stress factor for families.

My earliest research into supporting families (Burke and Cigno 1996) unfortunately indicated that living with childhood learning disability had for a number of families not reached the position of internalisation or adjustment as theorised, and one family had been caring for their child for 17 years, and rather achieved a plateau of adjustment at an earlier stage of transition. The reason was simple: living with the learning disability constantly produced difficulties for the family, whether to do with caring, schooling, sibling relationships or accessing scarce resources, such that the opportunity to reach full adjustment was never possible. My view, confirmed by recent research into siblings of disabled children (Burke 2004; Burke and Fell 2007), is that families accommodate their situation but never fully adjust to it when social and educational experiences reinforce difference, such that social exchanges become a constant challenge.

Needing help

The need for help and assistance in the families surveyed (Burke and Cigno 1996) was overwhelming; over 60 per cent of families indicated this need. Support, in its various guises, was often mentioned as a necessary lifeline, particularly for families at times of crisis (21 out of 35 responses).

Practical difficulties associated with caring for a disabled child reported in the returned questionnaire showed that transportation was the single most awkward factor in following family activities (over 70%: 37 out of 52 responses), followed by inviting friends home (27%: 14 out of 52). 'Doing things separately' was a factor which militated against family unity, especially with arranging holidays, for 7 out of 30 in the same grouping. Fortunately most families did manage to facilitate activities for their non-disabled children (93%: 42 out of 45), even though the disabled child might experience greater restrictions due to the difficulties mentioned (in terms of mobility, transport and access).

Despite some gains, it appears that looking after children with disabilities is restrictive for most families owing to the attention required, and for a substantial minority this restriction meant that paid employment was not possible.

Parental awareness and sense of difference living with disability

Parents were asked, within the format of the second study questionnaire, about their experiences and views concerning their children. This was necessary to identify the sense of a family's attitude toward their child with a disability. A change in attitude might well be expected to begin at the time the child is first recognised to be different.

It was interesting to discover how families perceived themselves as being different from others. The matter was addressed specifically by asking questions about whether the child's experiences were different from other children in the family, and whether life would be different without a disabled child. A further question asked about the *positive* effects of caring for the disabled child, necessarily focused toward the encouraging factors of living with disability to detract from any negative bias which might be construed within the preceding questions.

In reply to the first question, 41 per cent of children with disabilities were reported as requiring constant supervision or full nursing care. A further 32 per cent of parents experienced a sense of restricted freedom due to the demands of caring for the child. In other words, nearly three out of four children with disabilities required an intensive input of care and attention from their parents. Yet, one-third of the same group of parents were keen to point out that they treated all the children in the family exactly the same, despite that fact that the needs of the most disabled children were often considerably greater than the needs of their siblings. This appears to be representing intent rather than reality (but see Chapter 6 on the relative neglect of siblings). One parent expressed the experience of difference as follows: 'My disabled child requires closer surveillance or "looking out for". I have to be more watchful at bedtimes, bath times and making sure medication is taken. Everything takes longer.'

The response to the second question, from 46 families, showed that nearly half (21) felt that life without a disabled child would be less restrictive, while more than one in four (11) felt they might be able to seek paid employment if they were not having to meet the caring demands. One parent explained: 'You need more structure, a clear routine, more time, and care night and day. You have to administer medication, monitor diets, and it is all physically and emotionally draining.'

In response to the third question, it was noted that caring for a disabled child is associated with an increased understanding of disability-related issues (12 families expressed this view), that the family was brought closer together (ten families), and a greater expression of 'love and caring' characterised the view held by a further ten families. Whichever way one considers these findings, it seems that most families have a dutiful regard for their disabled children and go to considerable lengths to ensure their needs are met.

Consequences of disability on the family

The above views, however, are seemingly inconsistent with the finding concerning the impact of disability on the family, because 74 per cent of families (31 out of 42) reported that they found it difficult to do things together owing to the needs of their disabled child. Over three-quarters of the sample (43 families) expressed this as meaning that parents simply had less time for the non-disabled siblings. The family suffered as a direct consequence because it was difficult or impossible to do things together (over 70%: 29 out of 41 responses).

If families find it difficult to do things together then one questions what alternative sources of help will assist them. In the second survey, 'mothers' and 'social workers' received equal mentions (nine each), followed by 'nurses' (six) and family, friends and GPs (four each), as sources of potential help. Interestingly, the 'most helpful people' seemed fairly equally balanced between informal helpers and formal health and welfare services; within the general population this 'need' for networks of help might not be so critically drawn when families are not divided in sharing attention within their members. Secondary lines of support were also mentioned, particularly 'respite care' (five responses), which tended to echo family or friends or professionals as a back-up to the first mentioned helper.

It seems that living with child disability is reflected by families turning to variable networks of support, whether via friends and neighbours or through formal support networks. There seemed little differentiation between the types of support sought, so in speculating about the needs of families with a disabled child it is possible to suggest that the likelihood of including professional avenues of support is probably considered more as a back-up to normal familial support. The difference is that 'normal' families might not necessarily consider the need for professional help, whereas families with a disabled child routinely will.

Mothers' caring and employment opportunity

In the first study the main respondents were predominantly female (Burke and Cigno 1995, p.16) – 51 out of 67 respondents (76%) – contrasted with nine questionnaires completed by men. In the second study where results can be directly compared, 49 respondents out of 56 (90%) were identified as female compared with five completed by men (Burke and Montgomery 2003, p.12). In the first sample, nine women were lone parents compared with seven in the latter group. The results demonstrate what clearly appears to be a significant role for women as the primary carers of their children. While men might be expected to participate in the caring task, the primary responsibility appears to be with women.

While some questions were not always answered, it was possible to identify that women tended not to be in paid employment. In the first survey, 26 women were full-time carers compared with 33 in the later study, representing 39 and 58 per cent respectively. In the first survey, some 43 per cent of women (22 out of 51) were employed, compared with 33 per cent (16 out of 49) in the later study; the remainder were full-time carers. Expressions typical of mothers who felt their lives were restricted included the following:

- 'I could have continued working. There is so little personal time for myself and my husband and it is both physically and emotionally draining.'

- 'I would have followed a different path in life. I would probably be working instead of being at home.'

- [With a more positive twist] 'Perhaps more freedom but in many ways less enriched.'

This suggests that not all women carers have the option to follow employed work. For three families in the first survey and eight families in the second, neither partner was employed.

The cost of caring

It appears that child disability changes the employment possibilities within the family. This is particularly evident when women carers cannot occupy full-time work, so income is less for the family as a whole compared with families where both partners can be employed. Indeed, it has been reported that the cost of caring for a child who is disabled increases the childcare costs threefold (Dobson and Middleton 1998). The fact that a high proportion of women carers have reduced employment prospects further stresses the family income such that child care is effectively under-resourced at a point when costs are comparatively higher than for other families. Emerson and Hatton (2005) estimated that families living with a disabled child were 1.45 times more likely to be living in poverty and were 50 per cent more likely to be in debt compared with other families. The need to recognise the stress of financial difficulties and access to appropriate helping services is paramount.

Lone parents

It was evident from earlier research (Cigno with Burke 1996) that lone parents with a disabled child may have their lone status due to a partner's difficulty in dealing with disability. One mother reported that her husband had left the family home during their developmentally delayed daughter's first year at school: 'He buried his head in the sand and I got little support. [Daughter] was affected and her younger brother had to have counselling' (p.74). In another case, the mother of two children, one with learning disability, reported how her relationship with her husband had broken down owing to the stress of dealing with disability. On separating, she looked after her disabled child and her husband looked after the non-disabled sibling.

Mothers who were the sole carer of their disabled child said that a lack of money and mobility were major difficulties. As reported by Cigno with Burke (1997), a mother of a 13-year-old said: 'I don't think transport is flexible enough with one-parent families that have no transport of their own especially if [you are] ill as a lone parent' (p.183).

Lone parents found it difficult to find support and became dependent on the social worker. One mother reported that she no longer had a social worker and did not know where to turn, suggesting that lone parenting with a disabled child should take into account the relative isolation of some families. Such experiences reflect the difficult times some families have in dealing with disability.

It appears that the main caring responsibility still rests with mothers despite help available within the family. Lone parents may have little choice but to manage on their own, and the research I have carried out suggests that a significant minority *choose* to be on their own in relative isolation even though recognising the need for service input and professional support. It is also the case that some families have a closer relationship because of their caring experience.

Parents caring together

It is not necessarily the case that disability promotes marital conflict and separation. A number of parents commented that their relationship actually strengthened in their resolve to bring up a child with disability. One parent commented: 'It taught us to be more compassionate about others. It taught us patience. We have more love as a family. Our experience has brought us closer together.'

In the first study the experience of parents working together is confirmed by the view of 11 respondents (16%) that they considered their spouse their main source of advice and support (Burke and Cigno 1996, p.61). In the third study, 13 respondents (22%) expressed the view that their family had been brought closer together as a result of helping each other with the caring needs of their disabled child. These findings are consistent with those of Baldwin and Carlisle (1994) and confirm those previously reported by Blackard and Barsch (1982). Taanila, Jarvelin and Kookonen (1998) indicated that half of the parents said marital relationships were closer, which, together with the above findings, serves to suggest that childhood disability promotes closer relationships in many families.

Although the evidence is of families remaining together, Emerson and Hatton (2005) found that the percentage of single parents caring for a disabled child was more than in the general population (30% compared with 14%). Consequently, it appears that caring for a disabled child polarises families as either sticking together and strengthening the relationship or separating to start a new life: diverse reactions to a given situation.

One family, this time still intact with both parents, expressed a caring responsibility for looking after their disabled son Simon, but presented the view that when Simon was at home everything centred on him and activities he was able to follow. His two brothers had to take a back seat experiencing relative neglect due to Simon's needs.

Fathers

In a study by Dyson (1997), it was shown that both fathers and mothers of disabled children experienced greater stress than did parents with non-disabled children. Britton's (2001) study found that fathers of disabled children need more support, a finding which echoed that of West (2000) and followed Carpenter and Herbert's (1997) recognition that fathers needed access to support including opportunities to meet other fathers. It appears that fathers do indeed share in the stress experience within the family in addressing the needs of their disabled child, reinforcing the need for a family perspective concerning the provision of services.

Dale (1995) questioned the situation of fathers, suggesting their status receives scant professional attention. Fathers may not receive the attention they deserve, although it is clear from the author's studies that men also act as the main carers. However, they remain a minority, representing nine carers in the first study and five in the second (16% and 8% respectively). Although this evidence is not conclusive, and shows variability between the two studies, it is clear that a proportion of men do assume a main caring role. Consequently, the need for service provision and professional support requires further examination. The professional social care worker should consider the whole family (including the father) when carrying out assessments relating to a child who is disabled.

Support from relatives

Extended families may provide support to the family with a disabled child. Meyer and Vadsey (1997) comment on the special status that grandparents have; but as Mirfin-Veitch, Bray and Watson (1997) explained, grandparents not only struggle to come to terms with a child's disability themselves but they also have to recognise the problems their own daughter or son faces. This can create difficulties for grandparents in providing support that is needed within the family.

However, despite recognising this potential for difficulties, some parents actually turned to their extended families for support. In the first study, 11 respondents (9%) did so; in the third study, nine respondents (15%) said their relatives were a main source of support. One parent said: 'Relatives are most helpful due to their support and trust my daughter has in them.'

It seems entirely natural that families turn to relatives for help and support, but families need additional help often beyond the ability of grandparents to offer, such as short-term respite care or basic help with household chores, particularly if the care needs of a child are considerable.

Service provision and professional involvement

The provision of services for families with disabled children would seem at face value to be an entitlement, especially given the emotional adjustments combined with financial implications associated with caring for a disabled child. An examination of the frequency of professional contacts when compared with the range of services provided, as has been demonstrated by Walker (2002), tends to be focused more on statutory protection concerns rather than on supporting the family by offering services of a preventative nature (see also Burke, Manthorpe and Cigno

1997). The range of service provision is regarded as a 'continuum of services' to support children and their families and is outlined in the *Framework for the Assessment of Children in Need and their Families* (DoH 2000a), so it is interesting to comment on the support that is available.

In my second study (Appendix, Figure A.1; also Burke and Montgomery 2003, p.15) the data showed that 17 families who regularly received professional support also obtained the services they required. The converse was also true for ten families who did not get professional support because they did not receive the services they might otherwise have expected. In other words, it is significant that regular contact with professionals helps access service provision, and that not keeping in touch with professionals means that service provision is not provided.

The reality is that families who do not find out what services are available – and these might include the most vulnerable families – will not access professionals to gain the services they need. These data indicate (within the limits of a small-scale study) that, while the welfare system may well help those who help themselves, the regular involvement of professionals improves access to services. It suggests professionals need to be more proactive when dealing with families who might otherwise tend to isolate themselves in the community. It should not be accepted that such families 'go it alone' because they are reluctant to avail themselves of services. It is clear that without contacting professionals the nature of service provision will not be known to service users, when an appropriate professional service provider could potentially make some situations resolvable – accessing grants (given financial issues for many families), respite care or other support services to help reduce stress.

Conclusion

Caring for a disabled child can be an exhausting 24-hour responsibility, and consequently some confusion may exist, within the family, about how needs can or should be met. My first study (Burke and Cigno 1996) pointed towards families needing a positive input from the service providers who should respond to and provide information and help when needed. Families also needed specialist equipment in some cases (Beresford 2003) and many still had problems getting the necessary adaptations quickly despite expert advice (Oldman and Beresford 1998), such that support needed to be followed by a plan to implement specific equipment needs, necessary to reduce some of the difficulty of caring.

Research by Beresford *et al.* (1996) and Murray (2000) showed that parents are empowered when professionals work with them. The opinions of the parent, if sought and valued, contribute to an under-standing of the needs of the child with a disability. There is a need for clear information from professionals about the services that are available, because research suggests that such information tends not to be provided (Mitchell and Sloper 2000; Ward *et al.* 2003).

Lack of additional support and resources results in further stress factors that tend to increase the elements of perceived stress because of the lack of support. Unfortunately, the most vulnerable families are those who try not to be any trouble and go it alone and so do not actively seek support. That should never be the case if working together with profes-sionals, and clearly issues of pride and self-determination need to be overcome when recognising the needs of the disabled child to give the child the best opportunity for the future. That sometimes means over-coming personal reluctances to seek support or help and to recognise it is the child's right to receive the optimum level of service that is available for them.

Practice notes

Is diagnosis important for identifying the nature of disability?
This is a complex field. Diagnosis refers to the medical view of disability, and it might more properly be considered to be about the diagnosis of an impairment, which concerns a difference in the functional or intellectual ability of the individual. The question then arises as to how the impair-ment impacts on the individual. It may be accepted without any form of medical intervention, or be augmented with some aid, for example, to assist hearing or sight, or mechanical aids when physical strength is lacking (as with arthritic conditions). Surgery may also be an option following diagnosis, but individual wishes, which may resist surgical procedures, should always be respected.

The actual impairment as experienced by a child will usually include a parental input. Diagnosis may seem all-important in ascertaining the needs of the child, which the child may well not question, accepting decisions made on his or her behalf. Such factors will influence the family's understanding and acceptance of the child when the more usual expectations for a non-disabled child have to be reframed.

What about suspicions that your child is disabled?
This concerns the time when 'disability' (the term usually used rather than 'impairment') is first considered by the family and whether it was suspected by the family at the prenatal stage, at birth or sometime later. Later diagnosis may occur in certain conditions, for example in children on the autistic spectrum, or with impairments not detectable at birth which may present as learning disabilities, sometimes even as late as secondary school. Families may find that a diagnosis helps them feel that they can then understand why they think their child is different, but the research shows that the child tends to be the family's first consideration, and when special needs are identified the family should be informed that specialist help is available. Social work is probably underplayed in this scenario, when medical help is often the first recourse, due to the diagnostic expectation.

What about the consequences of stress reactions?
The reaction to a diagnosed condition and the impact this has on living with disability for the family, in terms of their ability to deal with and understand their child's disability, will be influenced by the nature and understanding of the child's condition. Diagnosis may seem to be a passport to services and this view will reflect some conditioning towards a medical perspective centred on impairment without considering its impact in terms of social exclusion. Professionals may question whether social and environmental experiences create as much of a stress reaction as any diagnosed medical condition.

Should mothers and fathers always expect to undertake the caring responsibilities?
The reaction of families to the caring task depends on the parents. Some are strengthened by working together. For others, the mother may take on the caring role alone with an impact on her employment prospects and the probability of a lowered family income. Some family relationships are stressed and families split up, although most families in the research cited appeared to have a stronger supportive relationship. Many with positive views of disability counter negative perceptions, although

isolation from family and friends may be a negative indicator. Interestingly, non-disabled siblings will also offer support and be involved in caring tasks, a factor not all parents may recognise. Depending on the nature of disabilities, many families will require additional help, whether respite care, child-sitting services, or direct help in the home to be given a break from the caring responsibilities or to offer relief from the additional tasks in maintaining the home.

Is professional support needed?

This is about the assistance provided by health, educational and welfare professionals. Almost invariably some input is welcomed by families, although some may deny this need – whether this is due to a non-acceptance of disability or a fear that they, the family, will appear not to be capable of caring (with the consequence that their child needs care by others). It appeared that a number of lone-parent families were not actively seeking support, with the consequence that they did not get it. Clearly, the right to gain professional support should be recognised and parents and carers need to be made to feel that accessing services is not an indication of failing but rather is recognition that their caring duties need backing up – to help reduce the potential build-up of stress linked to heavy or unmitigated caring responsibilities.

Chapter 4

The Impact of Childhood Disability: Professional Understanding

This chapter continues to examine the research which suggests that living with a disabled child creates an identity with disability for all family members. This requires a professional understanding of the family so that families will be confident enough to be able to draw on the varying levels of support, assistance and services from welfare agencies. The impact on the family is qualified by case examination to show that living with disability appears consistent with certain experiences that are grounded in the concepts of attachment, change and resilience. A child-centred practice framework is applied to two case studies used to illustrate the family experience.

Attachments

The ability to deal with new experiences is evidently linked to the 'attachments' that a child makes in early childhood, usually to a parent figure (Bowlby 1951; Rutter 1987). Over a period, a child begins to react to friendly stimulation and learns within the first year of life to recognise a caring individual. Bowlby usually calls this person the mother, although 'mother' may be generalised to the individual of most significance in a child's early development. The theory suggests that making an attachment results in a good bond, such that a child with good attachment experiences would be expected to be able to form relationships with others. The child having learnt that the bonding experience is rewarding also finds that social interactions are likely to bring a positive gain to his or her own life. The impact of good attachment behaviours links with the ability to cope with changing situations, and the ability to manage difficulties, including overcoming adversity. Attachment will produce the coping mechanism needed to deal with loss in adult life, a view consistent with the research of Sable (1989).

However, individuals without a secure attachment (i.e. those who have not experienced caring during early childhood experiences) may develop defence mechanisms to deal with loss. Falhberg (1994) identified a range of attachment-related difficulties, including high anxiety, poor impulse control, a lack of positive self-esteem, low levels of trust, emotional problems, confused thought and physical or expressive problems. Put simply, attachment helps us to deal with events which can be anticipated (loss and bereavement being examples). But, it might be postulated, with unanticipated events (such as the birth of a child with a severe disability), poor attachments might follow a sense of loss or bereavement. Poor early attachments are indicated by varied problems in social relationships. Reactions to an unexpected event may be similar to the bereavement process, but due to our inability to know or predict certain types of situation, when they do occur they evoke defence mechanisms, as a form of protection against the uncertainty.

Defence mechanisms

It was suggested in Chapter 3 (referring to Hopson 1981, citing Holme and Rahe) that accumulating stressful experiences can impact on the individual to the point that he or she is not able to deal with the events causing the stressful experience. The nature of such an impact is of interest. Psychologists (e.g. Atkinson *et al.* 1990) tell us that coping with stress may be achieved through acquiring one or more of a number of defence mechanisms, without any necessary awareness of the process involved. Defence mechanisms are a form of avoidance, an unconscious handling of the stressing event. The varying forms include the following:

- *Repression* – an involuntary blocking-out of painful memories by pushing such memories out of the mind. This is different from *suppression*, which is a deliberate pretence that denies the recognition of one's desires.

- *Regression* – returning to a less mature state, or period in one's mind when a stressful event occurred.

- *Rationalisation* – finding an explanation or justification for an event (which may or may not be logical). It is about explaining an event in a way that seems more acceptable or reasonable.

- *Reaction formation* – acting in a manner that is the opposite of the emotion felt.

- *Projection* –a way of shifting blame onto others.

- *Intellectualisation* – the detachment achieved by dealing with the abstract, ignoring the emotional content of a traumatic situation.

- *Denial* – an avoidance of the reality that any change has taken place or that any difficulties exist.

- *Displacement* – finding another outlet for an intense emotion by redirecting that emotional energy into a different activity.

There may be some elements of overlap, for example that displacement could link to a reaction formation; although the point here is not to elaborate on the nature of defence mechanisms, merely to clarify that it is a natural reaction to try to overcome difficulties and stressful experiences. Defence mechanisms enable us to have time to readjust to a difficult reality such as trauma or loss.

The process of adaptation can partly be explained by preparation for change, which may be of some help to alleviate part, if not all, of the stress that undesired change brings about. According to Stroebe and Schut (1999), a grief reaction may arise between dealing with trauma and enables time off from dealing with the trauma. This produces a kind of oscillation between acceptance and denial of the event, as though testing out one's adjustment to the reality of the stress experienced – seemingly a kind of natural sedative effect. As part of our own defence reactions, this form of denial can have a restorative function. This fits the model of regression as an occasional emotional experience, when an individual relives in his or her mind a traumatic experience and may benefit from discussing the experience if receiving professional counselling.

The Holmes and Rahe transition scale showed that events other than bereavement might compound to increase the degree of stress experienced by the individual. This is not to say that families experience bereavement because a child has a disability, but to suggest that reactions to disability within the family may be stressful and lead to an unconscious defence strategy. This can take the form of family reactive strategies including the following: a denial that the child has a disability; a denial that additional help or support is required; or a denial that disability has made a difference. Indeed, denial is a natural process of adjustment after a life-changing event, so some form of denial is to be expected.

This is a point clarified by French (2004), a woman with a visual disability, who discusses how, because of her awareness of the needs of others, denied the reality of her disability to reduce the apparent anxiety and stress it caused others. French had previously discovered when she openly discussed her difficulties, doing so would prompt disappointment, disbelief and disapproval; but by pretending to see what she could not, she engendered a sense of 'normality' and acceptance that avoided spoiling the fun of others, who would collude with her pretence. French would be asked 'Can you see the colours of the rainbow?' She could not, but by a simple reply of 'yes' she gained approval from others. This is a form of denial but it is also part of interactive skills when dealing with others, putting on a 'brave face', facing one's own reality but not pushing it into the face of other people. It is exactly what resilience involves: adapting to situations without fuss and gaining approval in the process. It is a mechanism adopted by families who put the needs of others before themselves.

A defensive attitude provides a means for dealing with the uncertainty that disability brings to most families new to the experience of living with disability: uncertainty due to a lack of familiarity or understanding, particularly in the initial stages, of the consequences of disability on the family's lifestyle, social experiences, and the seemingly inevitable need for professional support.

Resilience

The capacity to deal with uncertainty is assisted by resilience. The definition of resilience favoured by Daniel, Wassell and Gilligan (1999) and used by Fonagy *et al.* (1994) states that resilience is 'normal development under difficult conditions'. According to Payne, Horn and Relf (2000, p.22) all young people have the capacity to adapt to different circumstances although individual differences in vulnerability and resilience influence the degree of adaptation that is possible. Gillman (2004) argues that children are shaped by a number of potentially harmful and protective factors: harmful equates with an element of risk, and protective factors include the situational support available within the family, suggesting that it is a combination of difficult and supportive experiences that develops resilience. Stroebe, Stroebe and Hansson (1997) argue that the implicit resilience of children may be overlooked in research that considers dysfunctional qualities rather than an accommodation of difficulties. Werner's (1990) examination of international research on the subject indicated that resilient children elicit positive reactions from others, because it was found that resilient children had good communication skills, were sociable and independent – meaning that resilience is also about the ability to manage difficult situations. It appears that resilience can be learned but it requires an earlier experience of attachment if the child is to develop the capacity to deal with difficulties and finds some form of resolution to such difficulties.

I have earlier described resilience in action (Burke 2004, p.86). Angela (12) reacts to her brother John (9) who has learning difficulties. She describes her behaviour with her brother like this: 'Sometimes I just grab him [in frustration if he is tormenting her with incessant questioning and an inability to understand the answers] and I turn it around and I then make a fight a game, he likes that and I've let off steam.' Angela allows herself to release her anger towards him but is able to control her anger at the instant of its expression and uses her anger constructively in recognition of his and her own limitations. Consequently, she displaces her anger in a positive way; indeed she may even receive praise for her actions.

This expression of resilience in the home has defensive characteristics, in allowing anger (a defence against frustration) to be expressed, and may transcend to familial experiences of social exchanges. The effect of stigmatising events that are a reaction by others to disability with which the family must contend constructs disability by association, because of interactive exchanges (Goffman 1963). This concerns the expression by those beyond the immediate family's experience of living with a disabled child, a factor that features in daily interactions and engagements that constitute social life. The nature of changing experience is therefore worth some further examination.

Change
Research shows that major changes induce stress because new experiences are often associated with challenge, uncertainty and fear of the unknown (Lazarus and Foulkman 1984). It is perfectly normal to experience an increase in stress when unexpected events are encountered.

Middleton (1999) argues that change can bring about a positive identity. Moreover, a positive identity is about feeling good about oneself, 'acquiring identities relating to race, gender, age and appearance' (p.127), such that an identity acquired as a disabled person should involve an acceptance and public affirmation of self.

This is also expressed by Wolfensberger (1998, p.119) who writes about 'adaptative identity' as a means for developing competencies in devalued groups, such that when a socially acceptable status emerges it reduces the sense of difference and stigma associated with the devalued status. This is rather like the implementation of the social model when disability is not viewed as an individual problem; rather the need is to ensure the integration and acceptance of people within the community.

Living with a disabled child will bring about a change of perceptions of what can and what cannot be done. This is illustrated by the following quote from a child's mother: 'Days out during the school holidays are hard won. I'm a non-driver and going to the seaside on the train is ok one-way but a nightmare coming back. The trains are always packed on returning home and it is very difficult managing my son's wheelchair.' The reaction to and insistence in taking a short holiday break demonstrates that this mother is aware of the difficulties involved but perseveres nevertheless. She adapts to her and her son's abilities to manage on public transport, recognising the difficulties but accepting the challenge for the benefit of a day out.

Change enables the process of adjustment to be accomplished: resilience is the capacity to make such an adjustment a positive experience. However, any adjustment is potentially stressful, so understanding the nature of stress helps an appreciation of the human condition.

Adjusting to transitional stages

Adjusting to accommodate the experience of being stressed produces reactions of a defensive kind which may vary according to the stage of 'bereavement' followed; that is, when the stress is sufficiently difficult to need overcoming. The process of overcoming high stress levels often results in transitional adjustments. For example, becoming a parent is a major transition, as is starting school, or indeed moving through childhood to adolescence.

The adjustment to caring for a child with a disability is a transition for parents, but the experience of living with a brother or sister with a disability may be a form of transition too, because differences are highlighted in the school playground. This is evident in the remarks which have been reported to me of the type 'Your brother is mental and so are you'. This is hurtful and may not be received with tolerant and mature understanding, but requires a resilient attitude toward the behaviour of others. Research shows that transitions of any kind will cause stress (Jones 1998) and, in certain situations, stress might be accommodated but the nature of the transition must be understood. However, resilience helps to explain why, when faced with apparently similar situations, people may react differently, and resilient people tend to deal with situations in a better way.

Resilience, therefore, is the ability to manage difficult circumstances. This is exactly the situation of both siblings and children with disabilities when, as I found, parents express the view 'They grow beyond their years', to explain the maturity and understanding that siblings of children with disabilities commonly share.

A child-centred framework to help understand the location of resilience was described by Daniel et al. (1999, p.61) and is illustrated in Figure 4.1. It consists of a vertical and a horizontal axis. The vertical axis shows that a child may be located on any point along a scale from vulnerability to resilience; a horizontal axis locates the child on any point from adversity to a protective environment. This positions a child in one of four possible quadrants. The resilient and protected child, qualities associated with being good at problem solving, represents the first situation (1) in Figure 4.1. The second (2) is the resilient adversely experienced child who confronts marital discord and seeks adult help. The third (3) represents the vulnerable adversely affected child with poor attachment at home at school and socially. The fourth (4) represents the over-protected child who is vulnerable.

My own approach to dealing with the child-centred framework is to suggest that the vertical axis corresponds to a line running from social exclusion to social inclusion, and the horizontal axis shows powerlessness to a powerful dimension (Burke and Cigno 2000, p.4). These are included within Figure 4.1. The benefit of the latter is that practice techniques can then be identified with the various quadrants as a starting point for professional intervention. In interpreting the needs of the child it is proposed that practice fits within the array of four practice types identified as self-advocacy, support, prevention and empowerment. All represent possible ways of offering a working model following an initial intervention and identification of the child and family's likely identity.

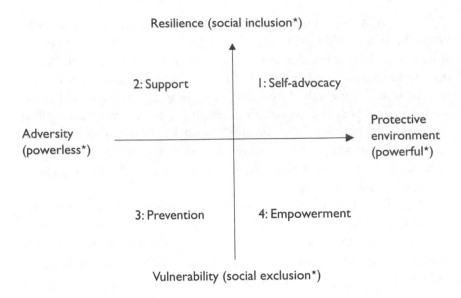

Figure 4.1 Child-centred framework – based on Daniel et al. (1999, p.61), and adapted from Burke and Cigno (2000, p.4*)

This suggestion is not intended to be absolute, but it is clear that an approximate fit, in terms of professional judgement, works for the model.

The vulnerable child

The most difficult situation represented in Figure 4.1 is in quadrant 3, when a child who is vulnerable and subject to adversity is consequently powerless and excluded. The preventive strategy at one extreme might necessitate removing the child from an abusive home to provide a protective environment. Research indicates that disabled children are at greater risk than non-disabled children. Figures vary, but Cross, Kaye and Ratnofsky (1993) found that disabled children are nearly twice as likely to be abused as non-disabled children, whereas Sullivan and Knutson (2000) in an American study found that disabled children were 3.4 times more likely to be abused or neglected. Sobsey *et al.* (1995) in an earlier study had suggested that the figures were even higher!

It is very clear that children with disabilities are more likely to be abused whichever evidence we cite. However, whether this apparent increased tendency to abuse actually reflects a predisposition to place disabled children on protection registers is unclear (Morris 1999), so the reality might be distorted to a degree. But the evidence remains, and the findings will no doubt link to the increased stresses experienced by families. Clearly, the need is for improved support services for isolated and vulnerable families. In the less extreme case, the need might simply lie in the offering of opportunities for expression to enable the child concerned to understand and make age-appropriate choices, a redirected preventive strategy with the intent of achieving some degree of resilience and protection, and enabling the child to become socially included and powerful.

Identifying the location of the child in the framework should help identify a way forward, perhaps by a concentration on increasing opportunities to develop resilience, typified by encouraging problem-solving skills. This may be achieved by focusing on reducing the experience of vulnerability faced by the child – for example, in the case of the powerless child with over-protective parents, the need for and enabling some element of greater freedom, certainly of expression, and introducing new experiences that promote choice. This requires support in quadrant 2 and is identified by an assessment. Individual cases do not necessarily fit the schema perfectly, but it indicates a point from which to begin.

It appears that a child-centred approach may help children if an opportunity is provided to encourage resilience behaviour within a safe environment. However, while such goals are laudable, sometimes the issues are more basic when related to children with disabilities, as the following case examples demonstrate. The point here is that in order to promote choice, an opportunity to question the nature of caring provided for a disabled child is fundamental to the achievement of higher aspirations. This cannot happen if the safe environment actually restricts opportunity, so the directional sense of the child-centred framework should increase opportunities.

Case examples

The following case examples are drawn from my earlier research (Burke and Cigno 2000) prior to developing a more detailed understanding of the implication of associative conditions. These cases are presented for the first time; they provide a focus on the situation of two families living with a severely disabled child. The examples illustrate how different support services are provided for similar situations (names are changed in all references to respondents and interviewees).

The case of John

John was born a healthy child but his mother had problems managing him and, at her request, John entered into the care of the local authority. Care proceedings were successfully initiated and John went to live in a foster home. After nine months of care, John had a cardiac arrest after choking on his own vomit. He suffered brain injury and was not expected to live. However, he slowly regained his health but had to be tube-fed and could communicate only by smiles and grimaces. He was diagnosed as spastic–quadriplegic and had little voluntary movement. He returned to his foster family on discharge from hospital.

The foster carers had initial difficulty managing John so, with social services support, a period of intensive rehabilitation at a specialist unit for children with acquired brain injury was arranged and the family began to learn how to manage John. He improved in his drinking and feeding skills because of rehabilitation and, although he was unable to speak, he appeared to enjoy watching television. His return home was planned following a major adaptation to the home and financial assistance with an enhanced foster care allowance for the family. The foster family maintained contact with the birth family and John had a comfortable home life.

Locus of control. In this family, the carers had an internal control. They were helped to arrange for the necessary adaptations to their home, following advice from the appropriate professional representatives, working closely with social care staff to ensure that the needs of both John and the family could be met.

The case of Matthew

Matthew was born healthy, but at the age of three he suffered a form of encephalophy after being treated for a childhood cancer. His adverse reaction to treatment left him comatose and he was not expected to survive. However, he slowly regained his health but had to be tube-fed. He began to communicate by smiles and grimaces. He was, like John, diagnosed as spastic–quadriplegic and had little voluntary movement.

Shortly before Matthew's fourth birthday he returned home with his newly born brother and the family resumed their life as well as they were able, given support from health and social services. Over the following five years, Matthew resumed oral feeding but continued to have communication difficulties and required intensive attention to his care needs due to sickness and immobility.

A major adaptation was necessary to the family home, which with a financial assessment of family income resulted in the provision of a special lift and bathroom and bedroom facilities. The similarities in the family's need paralleled John's situation, although the period for Matthew's family took longer resulting in a complaint by the family to the Ombudsman. The complaint was upheld and the local authority awarded the family a small amount of financial compensation and ensured the necessary aids were included with the adaptation provided in the home.

Locus of control. In this family the locus of control was external to the family as they waited for the needed adaptations to be provided by the local authority with the duty to assist. The Ombudsman returned some control to the family following an investigation into the delays, acting as an independent external agent.

Comment

John and Matthew appear to have similar needs, given high dependency on the support of their carers, a foster family and birth family. Both families seem to offer the best care they can and treat both young men as well as they can. This raised the issue of whether a child with a disability is better off within a foster family or the birth family. Attachment theory would probably advocate for the birth family, so that change is minimised. Nevertheless, attachment as an early learning experience is transferable, and if the birth family cannot manage then it might be agreed that it is in the child's interest to be cared for by a family choosing to do so. Either situation might be equally caring if the needs of the child are being met; the issue is whether the positions of the families are also equivalent.

The next consideration, therefore, might raise a question about the capacity of the families to care for the disabled child. In John's case, the foster family felt an obligation to care for him following his unfortunate experience which led to brain injury; similarly with Matthew's family, so both appear to be doing their best. However, the foster family were considered by welfare professionals as service providers while the birth family were viewed as service users. The former are paid for a service, the latter hold normal parental responsibilities and do not receive enhanced payments. Twigg (1989) identifies foster carers as formal carers and families as informal carers, reflecting a dichotomy between carers as professionals and parents as non-professionals, with a resultant resistance in power sharing (Foucault 1980, p.142) by welfare professionals in not treating both parties the same. Both families, nevertheless, will be entitled to welfare benefits associated with caring for a disabled person.

It is the differentiation between service providers and service users which raises the issue of whether each family is treated equally by welfare professionals. It is here that some differences appear to materialise between the two boys; services for the first include an enhanced foster carer allowance which the birth parents will not have. Perhaps that is what we might expect, except that John is offered access to specialist rehabilitation and Matthew is not, John is provided with a purpose-designed adaptation rapidly, Matthew is not (hence the Ombudsman's investigation) so it appears that professionals favour working and assisting professionals, fosterer carers are service providers as formal carers, parents are service users as informal carers. Thus, service professionals may treat birth families discriminatively because they may not realise the need to treat service providers and service users equally. It may be that a simple risk assessment indicates that a birth family will carry on in adversity, when the foster family may not. An alternative service provider may not be available, thus indicating that parental attachment outweighs considerations with professional service providers.

It could be pointed out that the two case examples are extreme and do not mirror current practice in any situation other than the examples themselves. Hopefully that is true; but with many expressions of good intent, practice cannot always be guaranteed to follow, and so these examples show how some differentials in service may emerge, and unless some comparative review is made, most professionals will not automatically be aware that such variations in resource provision actually exist.

Conclusion

Service provision is not the same for all families, and is probably avoided by some families reporting little use of services, thus posing the question: Is being labelled a service user a stigmatising experience? Apparently so, and avoidance is understandable, but the cost to the family is that families face increasing stresses in caring for a child with disabilities and may experience delays in service provision. All family members carry the anxiety of professional investigations given an identified need. They experience denial and a resistance to acknowledged need, despite encouraging qualities of resilience that might seem indicative of a capacity to deal with their situation. A child-centred framework super-imposed with an action-orientated practice typology helps to show that change is a process that needs to be acquired. Only then will profession-als begin to realise that people are not automata; they are all different, working at differing paces with prior experiences which make adjustment not so easy to accommodate.

Practice notes

Do early attachments make a difference?

Attachment refers to the bonding process that takes place between a child and its carer (often the mother) during the early stages of a child's development. In the case of children with disabilities, some parents said they felt they probably had a stronger attachment to their child before they knew about the child's disability; others who knew earlier on that their child was different simply felt they had accepted the child's disabil-ity from the outset and so their attachment was complete. Indeed, others found that the early detection of a disability (or more properly an impair-ment) caused mixed reactions, in the sense that familial expectations could not be met, so attachments were possibly impeded initially for these families due to uncertainties about the future quality of life for their child. It seems that all families are different in their reactions to child dis-ability and clearly early acceptance is an important consideration for child–parent bonding to take place.

Is it usual to experience negative reactions to disability?

It is not unusual to experience an initial reaction that tends to deny the reality of a child's disability, followed by some experience of negativity, probably due to the need to understand and begin to accept disability in the family. Partly this is because the parents or carers may find it hard to accept that their child has a disability which will most probably have a significant impact on themselves and other family members in the future. Changes in social attitudes may help overcome some negative views, and professionals may be equipped to assist such a progression.

Are some more resilient than others?

We are all different whether or not we have a defined disability or impairment. The capacity to deal with problems and the ability to make the best out of difficult situations is called resilience, or 'normal development under difficult situations' (Fonagy *et al.* 1994). This seems to be the case for disabled children and their families; enabling the development of resilient qualities is helped by offering opportunities to make choices and to be involved in decision-making. Such provision helps people to express their individuality and to take responsibilities in a positive way.

Can families accommodate change?

New experiences induce some element of stress, and living with disability will require engagement with many professionals, such that a constant element of changing resources and provision may be experienced. This may push some families to cut off from professionals if they cannot cope with an excess of advice which they feel disempowers them and might seem impossible to act upon. The introduction of a lead professional under the *Common Assessment Framework* should reduce some of the initial reactive tress that is experienced by families.

What are transitional states?

Any adjustment that is required to achieve change is a transition. This can be in attitudes to and acceptance of disability, or may be due to a change of school, a move to a new situation, etc. Professional assessments will sometimes speak of transitional statements to show a plan to accommodate a change due to schooling needs and the move from secondary education to further caring or other educative provision.

What is a child-centred framework?

This is about a professional assessment designed to recognise the transitional adjustments a child may need to accommodate, defining his or her need for protection and capacity to accommodate inclusion. A child-centred framework puts the child's needs central to the family's. Such frameworks may require certain procedural practices, as with the Common Assessment Framework, which is designed to enable a degree of prescriptive investigation when identifying the needs of children. However, procedural guidance alone cannot always ensure that correct professional judgements follow, but should demonstrate that decisions made were based on information gathered for the assessment. Once service needs are determined, any gap in service provision resources can be identified, falling into the catch-all category of 'unmet needs'.

Is there a child protection need for disabled children?

Children with disabilities are, according to the statistics, more likely to be abused than non-disabled children (figures vary from twice to nearly four times more likely), so it is imperative that we understand why this is so because a protection issue clearly exists. This may be a reflection of the additional stress on families and a tendency to over-react, but it may equally mean an over-representation and willingness to label disabled children as abused. Whatever the reality, the need for preventive services is clear, and isolated families especially need help rather than being subjected to the experience of exclusion from service provision. It is also clear that abusive situations cannot be condoned. However, the danger is that ignoring family needs will aggravate stress in family situations where caring responsibilities seem relentless, and such families need professional support.

Chapter 5

Support Across Early Life Transitions

The experience of transition and change is an expectation in any child's developmental progress: starting and leaving school, and leaving home and moving toward some form of independence from parental care. Transition is examined in this chapter, reflecting a move from dependence to independence, the latter often involving moving away from home. For the disabled person a move from home may not be entirely novel, because the nature of family support will, by the time school leaving transitions have been considered, have utilised care beyond the immediate family including school attendance, respite care periods or short-term breaks. It is within a framework of transition that a family learns to adjust to life experiences and change and the child-centred focus of attention needs to move to adult-related deliberations.

In order to appreciate the impact on the young disabled person and family, this chapter explores what happens during the transitions the young disabled child experiences in growing up and achieving some independence from the family carers. In particular, there is a coming to terms in the adjustment of the family's understanding of their 'child's' needs as a young 'independent' adult but possibly still dependent on others for a range of personal care needs. Indeed, the family may still fail to recognise the need for some form of independence for their perceived 'dependent child'.

Independence, interdependency and dependency

Independence is about deciding and doing things for oneself. In the case of a person who has a degree of impairment some things might not be possible and so a dependency might be created; but this is not necessarily so especially if the person has control over the process of being helped to be independent. Oliver (1990) argues that control of one's life is a basic right, and when an individual is dependent, self-empowerment represents a means to gain control.

In normal childhood development there is a natural progression from dependence through interdependence to independence.

- Dependency is when one individual relies on another for nurturing and care.

- Interdependence might be thought of as a sharing process whereby some control is handed to or assumed by another but the arrangement has some element of reciprocity.

- Independence occurs when one takes full control of one's actions and relationships. Independence may be in some sense artificial, as social cohesion requires some dependency on relationships, and particularly the institution of family, as a means for maintaining our lives.

In a basic example, a child will conform to family mealtimes or routines, accepting that because their parents determine decisions about meals there is compliance due to a dependent relationship. This is, of course, an overly simplistic representation of what happens; some families may not sit down to meals at all. However, the point is clear, that interdependence is about sharing some responsibility, and in following that responsibility parents might often assume that transferring the right to make choices is a transitional process for one's children.

Transitions

In discussing transitions, Burke and Cigno (1996, p.114) make the point that, while each case is different, there are broad areas of similarities in the experiences of families with disabled children as life stages are encountered. It was demonstrated that, although descriptive accounts make normative assumptions, they help to typify experiences of others and consequently aid our understanding of experiences encountered through schooling and later life stages. The 'phasing' as described by Hopson (1981), or in relation to reactive stages as utilised by Burke (2004, p.30) on bereavement, have in common the sense of progressing from one reactive stage to another in the process of adaptation and acceptance of a change.

McNair and Rusch (1991) demonstrated that parental support is vital for young people with learning disabilities in achieving a successful outcome, through the process involving the transition of a son or daughter from child to adult. Powell and Gallagher (1993) stress that parents need to talk and explain their plans for their disabled child with other children in the family. This view is supported by research by Hendy and Pascall (2001) which showed that for disabled people aged 20 to 30 parental involvement is an important resource in the transition process to independence. They may require help with this. With some resolution or acceptance of the child's disability, and the child's need to gain a degree of independence (initially), will also come a greater sense of achievement. It may point toward an independent future. Professional alertness to these needs should be part of a practitioner's repertoire of helping knowledge and skills. A stage in the direction of independence may be achieved by utilising respite care.

Support for children with special needs

The earlier work by Burke and Cigno (1996) and later Burke (2004) indicates that families with disabled children appear to plateau in their reactive stage to living with and understanding the needs of a disabled child. This is because daily encounters with individuals, family, friends and professionals often result in a defensive reaction to such engagements which is short of an acceptance of disability, although it often results from a protective instinct toward the disabled child. This is understandable if parents, or indeed siblings, have to explain difference within the family to others, while an endless stream of 'others' makes the task wearisome. So one family may appear compliant whereas another battles with whichever and whatever experiences they encounter and re-encounter.

The case of Sarah

One consequence of caring for a disabled child may be a sense of isolation for the family. This was the experience of Sarah, aged 11, (Burke and Cigno 1996, p.118) whose mother lived with her disabled daughter and had minimal family and social contact at weekends due to the high-level 24-hour routine of meeting the caring needs of her daughter. In the week both had their respective roles, mother as a part-time teacher's aide and daughter as pupil at a special school; but from 4.40 on Friday afternoon until 8.30 on Monday morning they were effectively trapped in the home. It is a fact that mum could push Sarah in her buggy, get out and go to the local shops, but the buggy was large and heavy and excursions out of the house were difficult and consequently rare. So what are the solutions to such problems and have matters changed since the earlier study nearly a decade ago? What are the choices?

Comment

The sense of dealing with day-to-day matters was all that Sarah's mother could comprehend, such that future prospects seemed remote and unrealistic. Consequently, professional involvement is imperative if we are to begin to identify when the time for change is right, because a daughter's independence is a vital consideration. This is particularly important if both mother and daughter are to achieve some degree of independence as each gets older. The need to move forward is a transitional passage, which most families experience as children grow up and take on adult responsibilities, but is all the more difficult if a disabled child has high dependency needs like Sarah. Many parents do not accept separation as a way of achieving independence, although some elements of separate living experiences might be in the best interest of both parties.

The case of Julie

The following case was first reported in Burke (1998, p.105) and is re-examined here regarding the transitional adjustments which were evident following an interview with Julie's mother.

At the point of interview Julie was 13 and living with her mother on a council estate in a remote village. Mother and father had separated a year earlier with father caring for their son, aged 17, while mother cared for Julie. Julie has learning difficulties but at 13 she can dress herself. She cannot read or write and has limited verbal communication. Julie attends a special school and is a weekly boarder, returning home for the weekend; occasionally, approximately every six weeks, she stays at the school hostel for the weekend. This means her mother can work during the week but has to be available at all times when her daughter is at home for the weekend. Without her partner to support her, mother finds caring for Julie difficult at the weekend and accepts that Julie will probably have to move into some type of protective institution in the future. Mother cannot imagine that Julie will ever achieve full independence due to her vulnerability: she considers Julie to be 'easy prey' for anyone wishing to take advantage of her. Mother also has cancer and so feels forced to consider alternative care arrangements for her daughter but intends delaying this as long as they both can manage with the existing arrangements.

Comment

The case of Julie illustrates several factors that impinge on the carer's role. These concern a sense of isolation from informal sources of help, including family and friends, and a dependence on services that are provided for families with children with special needs (education facilities accessed via a Statement of Special Educational Needs). However, the case is different from many. With the departure of her partner combined with caring for a disabled child, the diagnosis of cancer forced Julie's mother to face the realisation that one day she could no longer care for her daughter herself. The transition has in part been assisted by the fact that the special school is able to take boarders during the week and offers weekend respite care at its own hostel. The latter is based on the premise that a 24-hour curriculum would enable Julie and other residents to maximise their educational potential, while offering valuable respite to mother. Time away from home is one way of adjusting to the fact that their children, like others, grow up and have a right to an independent life; albeit that in Julie's case some caring responsibilities may always have to be accepted by others.

School

Local authorities have a duty to identify children with special needs as a requirement within the Education Act 1996 and modified by the Special Educational Needs and Disability Act 2001. This may result in a Statement of Special Educational Needs (SEN) as clarified in the Code of Practice (DFES 2001, para. 1.3). This statement may result in the child attending a special or mainstream school, but special provision may be necessary according to the statement recommendations. It is now unlawful for institutions to treat disabled people less favourably than non-disabled people.

It is argued by Vaughn and Schumm (1995, p.265) that all students can receive an education in a general classroom (mainstream) unless their social needs cannot be met, warning that students with learning disabilities may not fully participate in mainstream classes. The evidence from Thomas and Pierson (1995) is that mainstream schools could meet the needs of 90 per cent of children with special educational needs. Oliver and Barnes (1998, p.42) argued that the numbers of children out of the mainstream was, at the time, increasing because of unnecessarily segregating children with special educational needs. However, the situation is changing and according to the BBC News (Education):

The government has promoted the idea that where possible children with special educational needs should receive help within a mainstream school. The intention is to give special needs pupils a greater sense of integration, rather than being taught in separate special schools. (BBC News, Education 2007a)

This follows a considered view that children with special needs should have the opportunity of inclusion within mainstream education. A reflection of this policy in action is that, in 1983, there were 1562 special schools in England compared with 1160 in 2003. The numbers of children with the most severe needs who are in mainstream schools had gone up 49 per cent in a decade (BBC News, Education 2007b).

However, it would appear that one solution does not fit all situations, as indicated by Thomas and Pierson (1995). Indeed, whichever school a child with special needs attends, it is worth noting the caution identified by Middleton (1999) that education should be beneficial. She states: 'Special education is evaluated less on its contribution to the needs of its pupils than on its contribution to the education system as a whole' (p.45). In other words a child with special needs may not benefit from an education system that does not meet the child's needs within a system that concerns the majority.

Study findings

In the third study initially reported in Burke and Fell (2007) there were varied responses to questions about school experience. One parent was less than satisfied with mainstream, explaining that there was an acute sense of discrimination in the school from other parents because of 'their attitudes to disability – parents verbally attacking you for your child's problems and poor achievements'.

Despite some negative expressions most parents found that sending a disabled child to school (mainstream or special) acted as a form of respite care for the family. Teachers were generally considered a source of support for families, for 16 per cent of families (11) in the second study and 25 per cent of families (25) in the third study. Teachers were accessible and valued for advice, as one parent explained: 'Teachers keep an overall eye on things because they are with the children for a good part of the day.' Another parent explained the special attention her son received at school like this: 'At school, he had his own entourage – two school helpers and a nursing assistant. Not only staff help, because when he started all the kids would follow him around – he was special you see' (Burke and Montgomery 2003, p.19).

Not all parents were concerned about the differences that their child experienced at school, as one parent explained: 'You experience the same pride when a certificate is brought home, the same concerns about whether school meals are eaten, and the same pleasure when your child makes a new friend.' It seems clear that most school experiences were positive and a valued source of support for families as well as providing care for the child during the day.

Other types of support requested by families with disabled children included the need for a child-sitter service alongside the need for short-term or respite care.

Child-sitter service

This is a specialist service provided by a sitter who has training in disability matters and will therefore not be fazed by children with varying disabilities. Baldwin and Carlisle (1994) showed, as did Burke and Cigno (1996), that the service was one preferred by families because it fell short of taking the child away from home. The service may be provided by voluntary or statutory agencies under s17 of the Children Act 1989. Sitters are available until the child reaches adult age, and as such are not the same as the conventional 'baby sitter' because of the specialist service that may be offered to families, including sitting for adolescents with special needs. Practical assistance with caring tasks, including dressing, feeding, toileting and generally assisting the child or young person, was considered to be needed by all families with disabled children. Siblings of disabled children (in the third study) were often used as substitute sitters (20%, 12 siblings) or in providing help with caring tasks (30%, 18 siblings), thus relieving parents of some elements of their caring role.

Respite care

Respite care means providing care for the child away from the family home so that the rest of the family might have a break; it is, in part, recognition that caring for a child with a disability may be emotionally and physically draining for the family. Indeed, Pitkeathley (1995, p.2) commented on carers being 'pushed to the limits of endurance'. A research report from the Joseph Rowntree Foundation (1999) indicated, perhaps not surprisingly, that parents appreciated breaks from their caring responsibilities. This positive experience of short-term breaks is backed by the earlier research of Beresford *et al.* (1996), although Middleton (1999) suggested that offering short-term breaks to disabled children discriminates against the disabled child in a way that does not impact on non-disabled children, because parents might emphasise their child's impairments to gain access to services. However, this may be more about the need for services and the desperation of parents to receive a break. Indeed my own evidence suggests a reluctance to accept services (see Chapter 4).

Other evidence suggests that respite care fails to support relationships (McNally, Bne-Shlomo and Newman 1999) or creates additional stress for those concerned (Hartrey and Wells 2003). Further, Connors and Stalker (2003, p.79) report that half the children in their 25-family research sample had short-term breaks, but noted that 'parents and children were rarely satisfied with the short break on offer'.

The respite care available may range from residential to foster care and day care. It may be provided by schools with hostel accommodation, be health-related, or provided by social service departments. With the latter, access may require the child being admitted into the Looked After System as part of the legislative route for placing a child if accessing foster care or residential provision provided by social service factors which will not impact on health or school provisions in the same way, and where parental agreement will often suffice.

This suggests that respite care can be extremely varied in style, so can it be concluded that it is not satisfactory? Indeed, that would appear to be the case, yet its continuation suggests that the need exists for its provision, indicating that the nature of respite care needs clearer coordination and organisation rather than not being available at all.

The evidence from Griffiths (2002) and from my own research (Burke and Cigno 2000) contradicts the more negative views expressed above. Parents were unequivocal in their praise of respite care; indeed the mother of Matthew said: 'I only fully realised how much I loved Matthew when he was away from home – then I could rest, so when he returned home I welcomed him with open arms' (Burke and Cigno 2000, p.141). In my earlier survey (Burke and Cigno 1996, p.62) five families that used the respite care service indicated that it provided them with their main source of support. The need for respite care also raised concerns for the disabled child's uncertain future. One parent expressed this very clearly: 'I worry about the future for my son. I know I will be there for him. I hope he will have some independence not just for himself but for myself too – who knows?'

Perhaps the arena of my own research shows that respite care can work; it is clearly needed by the families encountered, so when it is organised well it will benefit those involved. Also, despite some contra-indications to its beneficial effects, the service continues to be provided – so the clue here is more to do with the quality of available respite care combined with its continuity and sustainability rather than any sugges-tion to remove a precious resource.

Hospice care

A child with a disability may have a life-shortening condition. Short breaks for the family as a unit may then be provided by the hospice movement (Burke 1991). This care may involve all family members or be for the child alone, depending on family wishes and needs. The caring skills of the hospice staff will be able to deal with the difficulties families encounter and provide all with a break from everyday responsibilities. Staying in a hospice with a disabled and ill child will mean that parents do not feel the guilt of separation, and the experience may help them to come to terms with others taking on a caring responsibility. Planning breaks may help increase the caring capacity of parents at other times in other forms of respite care.

Meeting needs

A range of services should be identified which suit a particular child and family. Morris (1998, p.10) described a rights framework for young disabled people which should include 'the human right to a review of the placement at regular intervals'. Similarly, Hudson, Dearey and Glendinning (2005) wrote about a 'vision' that includes a comprehen-sive approach to accessible services that are tailored to individual circumstances. This follows aspirations raised in the Green Paper *Every Child Matters* (2003) which puts children first, and with services working together to meet needs.

Research by Franklin and Sloper (2007) shows that disabled children and young people should participate in decisions which concern them. This means expressing their voice in whatever way it can be heard, especially when not all disabled young people are able to communicate verbally. This may require special training for professionals, and recognition that speech might sometimes need augmenting with special aids for certain individuals. Perhaps, in determining needs, which seem all so clearly identified and articulated by many of the families interviewed, a professional social care worker should communicate with the disabled child to ensure that service provision covers his or her expressed needs. Services might include sitting arrangements, to longer-term options where respite care might be a bridge to possible future independence for the disabled child, or indeed it might exclude such possibilities and identify others.

The case of John, Amy and Allan

As reported in Burke and Cigno (2000, p.80), John (9) and Amy (6) share their home with Alan (13) who is believed to be autistic and has learning difficulties. Alan also suffers from mild epileptic fits and he can behave erratically if out with his family, causing them some discomfort mainly due to negative reactions from the public who look disapprovingly, especially if Alan is making too much noise or is not behaving compliantly. Alan's medical and educational needs were under further investigation at the time of the interviews with the family and were the cause of shared family anxiety. All the family believed that they benefited from the fact that Alan is a boarder at school during the week, returning home for the weekend only. This leaves more time for family activities that include John and Amy.

Comment

The children's mother reported the impact of her son's disability on her daughter's social life: 'People are less willing to invite her to a party because they don't want her brother there in case he has a fit. This means she gets invited out less.' This is a stigmatising experience that is situational because the child is excluded from a social event, but it is also associative because the apparent fear is that Amy will bring her brother with her to the party, suggesting that if Amy did not have a brother with a disability there would not be a problem in offering her an invitation.

John and Amy enjoy playtime with their brother and tolerate his different behaviour and, as noted previously (Burke and Cigno 2000), 'sibling relationships often manifest a natural acceptance of their brother or sister' (p.81). The acceptance demonstrated by John and Amy indicates a high positive form of reactive behaviour (Burke 2004, p.33). This might also be a feature of the fact that Alan is their older brother and both younger children grew up accepting him as he is, not questioning his different needs and behaviour. It is also significant that the family have regular breaks, due to the school routine, allowing time for activities with other family members. There is a need, however, to question the desirability of Alan's life away from home (if this is an option), and whether the family would be as well adjusted if the regular breaks were shorter.

In all probability, the family functioning may depend on these periods of time when Alan is at school, for without them the stresses could change the current playtime to more aggressive activities, increasing stress on the family. It is not certain that this would be the consequence; but if advocating a united family life, an element of social exclusion (for Alan) should not be the only answer. The reactions by the family to their perception of disapproval from the public, and avoidance of party invitations, suggests that the experience of Alan's disability is indeed stigmatising, such that acceptance is only partial, at home, and not necessarily so in other settings. Perhaps, as for many people, it is easier to avoid than to confront situations that create stress because of a fear for the consequences.

Locus of control. In this family it seems that situational events act as an external locus of control – whether it be the fear of a reaction by other children if including Alan in a party invitation, or in the provision of regular breaks offered by the education authority. The family have effectively become passive recipients subject to the controlling influence of another: a situation barely questioned by them when making decisions for the future which seems to be in the hands of external influences.

Sibling caring responsibilities

Siegal and Silverstein (1994) indicate that when a child takes on a caring role, he or she adopts one of several coping strategies. Through being a caregiver as well as a son or daughter, the child forms an alliance with the parents. According to Mayhew and Munn (1995), who ran a group for siblings of children with special needs, the siblings' role of carer gives them some status in the family.

School-aged siblings may themselves develop behaviour problems, indicating the need for teacher awareness and training. Jenkinson (1998) found that negative attitudes at school tended to stereotype siblings as different from their peers, and identified the fault as a lack of training given to teachers. Siblings face difficulties at school, find it difficult to bring friends home and suffer loss of self-esteem (Dyson 1996). The association with a disabled brother or sister can be stigmatising (Frude 1991), making it difficult for them to form attachments with other children at school. This partly reflects the reality that many children have never come across disability at close quarters and do not know how to cope with it. Children also, of course, reflect their parents' attitudes to disabled people.

Coping strategies are necessary, and status increases the level of self-esteem. However, the extent of the adverse effects of being a care-taker are not to be underestimated, for it is unlikely that these children will escape some negative effects of their caring role both at the time and/or at some future point in their lives.

The motivation to take on the role as caretaker can be less than straightforward, and siblings might not be aware of their motives. According to Seligman (1991) this is due to the child feeling a sense of guilt at not being disabled. This reflects the concept of survivor guilt following bereavement. It appears that siblings of disabled brothers and sisters may experience a sense of bereavement because they have to cope with the sense of loss due to their brother or sister's disability. Seligman (1991) also suggests that guilt is a strong motivating factor in overly helpful caring behaviour.

Conclusion

It is clear that living with a disabled child presents a challenge and a con-tinuing state of transition for families. Not all families have the same needs, so it is necessary to identify the nature of services that are required. One major benefit of providing a sitter service, schooling and short-term care is that carers have time for themselves at a point when their disabled child may be gaining new positive experiences. Such expe-riences may enable the acceptance of a future move from dependence on parents as carers towards the acceptance that others can do so, perhaps even achieving a point of independence for the child with disabilities when a suitable supportive framework of care is in place.

Practice notes

What do we mean by independence, interdependence and dependency?
Independence is the ability to care for oneself alone; interdependence is
caring for oneself but requiring some help from others, perhaps within
the family; and dependence is the need to have somebody to care for you,
as in the case of a young child. If someone is dependent, it does not
follow that he or she cannot make choices, and sometimes the ability to
make choices increases as independence is achieved; but most people,
whether or not they are disabled, will make choices which others will
implement on their behalf – that is interdependence.

What kinds of support are available?
Often support means professional support, when a professional worker
accesses services for a family and offers advice or simply listens. All
elements of support tend to be enabling of the person to whom some
form of professional help is offered.

Examples of support services include *child-sitter services,* which
involve a professional carer visiting the disabled child's home and caring
for the child for short periods so that parents may have time out from
their caring responsibilities. This is different from baby sitting when
dealing with a younger child, and child sitters will usually involve a specially trained carer and will often include individuals who hold nursing
or child care qualifications, and all will be checked for their suitability to
undertake child care (including Criminal Record Bureau checks).

Another support service is *respite or short-term care,* which is similar to
a child-sitter service except the care is usually in a residential home,
hospice or foster care and will often involve overnight stays. Utilising
services will sometimes involve a transition or adjustment period
whereby child and carers will experience a staging process with an
increasing building-up of the service provision, often necessary with
many disabled children who need to become familiar with new experiences and locations.

*Is there anything particular which may help professionals to understand families
with children with disabilities?*
Listening and understanding are of vital importance in trying to understand family needs. Professionals do need to appreciate that families,
even the most loving, may find it difficult to come to terms with the fact

that some of their expectations for their child will not be realised. Questions will vary from family to family: 'Will he/she live, walk or talk?' or even 'Which university/profession/career will he/she choose?'

The adjustment may never be achieved for some families – their uncertainty is continuous. A behaviourally disordered or severely disabled child may need 24-hour attention and these families never seem to stop working. They will envy a professional able to finish work at 5 pm when their day seems never-ending. Never being able to leave a room without careful checking, nor leaving the house without a caring arrangement for their child, means it is difficult to separate the carer's life from the child's. Respite care in these circumstances is highly prized, and if the professional can glimpse the world of seemingly endless toil, they may glimpse the world of the parent offering what can be unrequited and unremitting care.

Chapter 6

Siblings of Disabled Children

This chapter looks at the impact of childhood disability on brothers and sisters in the family and examines the familial and social acceptance of siblings with disabled brothers and sisters. The need to consider siblings of disabled children is introduced within The *Framework for the Assessment of Children in Need and their Families* (DoH 2000a), which mentions 'the importance of the relationship between disabled children and their siblings'. The document has effectively been superseded by the *Common Assessment Framework* (DfES 2006b) which, with a focus on disabilities and children with complex needs, is seemingly more encouraging about the situation of disabled children. However, the document, which is in excess of 9000 words, mentions siblings only twice: once within the current family (p.16) and subsequently in connection with family relationship (p.31).

It is important, therefore, that siblings with a disabled brother or sister should be properly identified as having needs, especially in recognising the element of care siblings provide, the latter being a factor that is well documented by research evidence (Aldridge and Becker 1994; Beresford 1994; Bone and Meltzer 1989; Stalker and Connors 2004). It is all the more surprising, then, that siblings receive such scant attention with regard to practice assessments in subsequent policy documentation. This chapter adds a comparative element from my own research (see the Appendix for methodological details) to demonstrate that siblings continue to play an important part in helping parents with disabled children, and that the needs of siblings do require greater emphasis and recognition within the assessment stages of professional practice. Reviews of the research in this area help locate the focus of my own work, and should help the reader to appreciate the situation of siblings in the family.

Research on the needs of siblings

Research by Stalker and Connors (2004) showed that siblings usually accept disability as part of their 'normality' owing to growing up with disability and treating their brothers and sisters like most 'normal families'. Whether all families are 'normal' is an issue examined by Parker and Olsen (1995), who recognised the diversity of family life where caring for parents or siblings is sometimes a feature of young people's lives; but for our purposes we want to identify the perception of families and young people living with and caring for a disabled child.

Naylor and Prescott's (2004) research indicated some reluctance by siblings to acknowledge their own feelings about disability in the family, suggesting a need to encourage self-expression. It is possible that Naylor and Prescott's findings indicate a degree of ambiguity when contrasting their results with those of Stalker and Connors. It may be that if siblings are reluctant to express their feelings in interviews then a perception of 'normality' might be presumed. An understanding of the reason for these differences needs to be sought.

In *Brothers and Sisters of Disabled Children* (Burke 2004), it was shown that a number of non-disabled siblings perceive themselves as disabled simply by being a member of a family living with a disabled child. A follow-up study tended to re-affirm that siblings had a strong association with disability (Burke and Fell 2007). The nature of this perceived disability led to the concept of 'disability by association', which is a form of family ownership of the disabled child's impairment. It locates various positive and negative effects on the family.

The findings of Naylor and Prescott might suggest that, when siblings follow a form of least resistance perceived as reluctance, this is the result of an interview effect (not to express feelings). The research by Stalker and Connors could be seen to overemphasise the identity of siblings with their perception of normality. This chapter compares the findings from two earlier studies (studies two and three in the Appendix; Figure A.1) to consider whether disability by association is representative of situations reported by families and siblings themselves. The indications are that siblings do not perceive a sense of normality within their families or with peers, although they do appear accepting of their situation and possibly wish to minimise their perceptions of difference to gain social acceptance and familial approval. In one case example (Burke 2004, pp.93–95), it was shown that Peter effectively discriminated against his disabled brother, Ian, as a negative feature of disability by association by avoiding social relationships. Results suggest that living with a disabled child creates an identity with disability that is accommodated by all family members despite some negative perceptions being reinforced by social interactions in non-familial settings.

In addition to the earlier research, the effect of stigmatising events which construct disability by association is examined here and is viewed as a consequence of interactive exchanges (Goffman 1963) as explored in Chapter 2. This concerns the expression by those beyond the immediate family's experience of living with a disabled child: a factor that features in daily interactions and engagements that constitute social life.

Disability by association extended the social model of disability (Shakespeare and Watson 2002) by demonstrating that the identity of disability is not entirely in the possession of disabled people themselves, because we all share some element of social impairment, and disability may be reconstructed for other family members in their own social experiences. It is recognised that disability has the potential to socially exclude a disabled person from social interaction (as with the issue of spoilt identity in stigmatisation); consequently, as with mental illness, the family and siblings of the disabled individual experience an impact akin to that of the person with the disability.

Comparative findings from siblings' survey

Of the four studies reported in this text, two examined the needs of siblings (the second and third studies in the Appendix). For simplicity, in this chapter they will be referred to the *first* and *second* sibling studies.

Both studies reflect questionnaire data provided by parents followed by interviews with parents and siblings. There is a tendency to let parents speak for the siblings, although views from siblings are also recorded to illustrate their comments which may not always mirror those of the parents. Earlier work by Burke and Cigno (2001) recognised the need to include children and young people in decisions which concerned them, a view reiterated by Franklin and Sloper (2007) and a feature germane to the *Common Assessment Framework* (DfES 2006a)

In the first sibling study, over 80 per cent of parents (46 respondents) indicated that siblings shared in the care of their disabled brother or sister, compared with 75 per cent (45 respondents) in the second sibling study. These results seem remarkably similar. However, with slightly less similarity, some 70 per cent (40 respondents) of families in the first study said that having a disabled brother or sister brought positive benefits to the family contrasted with 90 per cent (53 respondents) in the second study. This difference reflects a much higher indication of benefits viewed by respondents in the follow-up research. There might have been bias in the second study through self-selection, although the view that siblings actually helped in caring for disabled siblings was confirmed.

Living with a disabled brother or sister

The experience of living with a disabled child was clearly beneficial according to a number of parents. Expressions of their views included the following:

> My children have qualities lots of kids don't possess. They are aware of disability, never judge other children's behaviour and appear mature, compassionate, tolerant and caring in general. They also have a natural defence mechanism towards disabled people, especially their own brother and sister.

> My son now understands that everyone is different. He can use his own judgement on people. He realised life is not a bed of roses and you have to work at what you want to achieve.

> It has taught them that you should treat disabled people the same as able-bodied people and that you do not need to be afraid.

Not only were siblings viewed positively, familial relationships were also viewed positively. One parent expressed this view:

> Caring for a disabled child brought us closer, taught us to be more compassionate about others. Taught us patience. Given us more love as a family.

Views expressed by parents of a less positive attitude towards siblings living with disability seem circumstantially based, and included the following:

> I feel they have not been allowed to have a childhood. Julie's disabled child problems make doing things so difficult we've been restricted as to what we can do.

> It puts great strain on the family unit and they've been restricted in what they can do, something I feel guilty about all the time.

> We don't receive any help with our other two children about how best to deal and help them cope with having a disabled sister and this causes us a great deal of worry.

The positives were somewhat outweighed by the negative experiences of siblings, as reported by their parents. However, some regrets were tinged with a very positive regard. As one parent expressed her daughter's view:

> She regrets he is disabled but has no regrets at having a disabled brother. She says, 'He is my brother and I don't regret having him as my brother'.

The survey evidence shows that nearly 68 per cent (38) of parents in the first study reported that siblings, at some point, expressed regret at having a disabled brother or sister. A near identical finding in the second study also showed that 68 per cent (37) families expressed this view – consistent results for both studies. A significant minority of families, ten in the first study (almost 18%) expressed entirely negative views about the experience of childhood disability compared with five (8%) in the second study.

Families in the second sibling study had, overall, a more positive view of disability compared with the first study participants. Possibly, the wider database of the second study with its low response rate is a reflection of a more positive bias because respondents were far more self-selecting than occurred in the more locally involved first study with the higher response rate. It is interesting to find, however, that shared care by siblings and a high incidence with expressions of regret were similar in both surveys, suggesting that disability impacts more often negatively than positively in terms of sibling reactions within the family.

Parental and sibling views of living with a disabled child

A number of parents expressed the view that siblings of disabled brothers or sisters have a restricting or limiting experience that impacts on their quality of life. The following are examples:

> My daughter finds her disabled brother irritating, difficult to talk to and embarrassing. This started around her being in year 6. She often deliberately provokes him and has sometimes wished he would leave home.

> I feel they have not been allowed to have a carefree childhood. It puts a great strain on the family unit and they've been restricted in what they can do, something I feel guilty about all the time.

> My eldest son has lost out by not being able to play football and participate in the usual kid type activities with his brother.

Siblings also expressed the experience of living with disability in this way:

> I am concerned about John's condition and his future, also in thinking that there is a possibility of me giving birth to a child with the same 'illness'. (18-year-old sibling)

> We cannot have sleepovers or watch TV in bed as our house must be quiet. We have missed family events and holidays due to illness. Some friends won't visit because they don't understand. (16-year-old sibling)

Another sibling, Paul from the first study, expressed this view:

> Life would be easier without her, but if I had a magic wand I wouldn't make her any different, otherwise she wouldn't be Victoria. I'd keep her the way she is, otherwise she could end up like Jenny [grinning as he mentioned his older sister's name]. (Burke 2004, p.88).

This was more simply expressed by another sibling:

> He's my brother and I don't mind having him as my brother. (12-year-old girl)

These views reflect both the positive and negative views of family life. Often acceptance is tinged with regret, as one sister spoke of her brother:

> Sometimes I meet my friends, and some are boys of my brother's age and I wonder, if John had not been disabled, he might have been like them, but I will never know that. (14-year-old girl)

Another young person said;

> I wish we could play football together: he can't use his legs. (15-year-old boy)

The nature of disadvantage expressed by families was reported in both sibling studies as mainly leading to restricted social activities. In the first study, 74 per cent (31 families) reported that they found it difficult to do things together (Burke and Montgomery 2003, p.12), which contrasted with 56 per cent (28 families) in the second study (Burke and Fell 2007). It is simply the case that caring for a disabled child impacts on the family's ability to organise opportunities to do things together, such as going to the pictures, shopping or even a day out. Inevitably siblings miss opportunities because the amount of available time for parents is limited.

Shared care by siblings

It is apparent that a positive attitude from parents about their disabled child has a significant impact on whether or not siblings are viewed as helpful in sharing the caring responsibilities. Most parents in both studies indicated that having a disabled child brought positive benefits to the family. A minority of parents indicated that there was little benefit in having a disabled child and that siblings would not help with caring responsibilities. Parental attitudes towards the disabled child seem to be mirrored in their view of their non-disabled children – a negative attitude about having a disabled child being associated with a negative view about the ability of siblings to help.

Whether or not a negative transfer took place, over two-thirds of siblings at some point expressed regret at having a disabled brother or sister. It seems that positive attitudes promote positive feelings, as might be expected, and the converse. This may be a pointer for professionals when working with families that see only the difficulties and not the benefits of having a disabled child.

Relieving the pressure on parents

The situation of brothers and sisters helping their disabled sibling is reflected in the following examples drawn from the interview stage of the research. In the morning Matthew (9) gets up a few minutes before his mother and gives his disabled sister her bottle, thus allowing his mother a few extra minutes of sleep. Another sibling, Alan (14), will take his younger disabled sister out of a shop when she has a screaming attack to enable his mother to get on with her shopping. Routinely Katy (13) accompanies her younger disabled brother upstairs to read him his bedtime stories. She said: 'I like being able to give my parents a chance to relax. You're the one who looks after him and that takes the pressure off mum and dad.' Another 14-year-old girl commented: 'I sometimes do the child-sitter's job, if my mum and dad need to go out together. John needs to be watched even though he is two years older than me.'

It is evident that siblings like to help because by doing so they take pressure off their parents. They play their part in maintaining relationships and in re-establishing the family equilibrium when that needs to be done. Tozer (1996) points out: 'Siblings seem to act both as carers themselves and as supporters to their parents, the main carers' (pp. 177–178).

Effect on sibling maturity

A common view of parents with a positive attitude is that their non-disabled children are forced to maturity earlier, displacing the opportunity for some of the more usual childhood activities in the process. The first sibling study found that two-thirds of parents who expressed a view (27 out of 40) thought that their non-disabled children were more caring and aware of disabilities. It certainly appears that siblings are aware that their situation is different from that of other children; they see that they are expected to help their parents.

Myers (1978) writes of the additional responsibility siblings of disabled brothers and sisters are given and how they are expected to mature more quickly. Powell and Ogle (1995) suggest that parents need to talk to their children about future plans for the disabled child, so that siblings feel included and understand parental intentions, rather than living in a state of uncertainty, not being fully aware or necessarily resolving their feelings of responsibility toward their disabled sibling. Indeed the point is made that siblings take on responsibility 'beyond what is normally expected in sibling relationships' (p.83).

It is unfortunate that a negative parental view appears to deny that siblings have the ability to be helpful. It may seem also to be a denial of more usual childhood experiences when siblings accept caring responsibilities, which otherwise require a specially trained sitter, and remain supported by their parents. It seems all the more difficult for siblings when the responsibilities they accept were not acknowledged by some of their parents.

Service delivery

An area of disquiet raised in the first sibling study concerned the contact between families and service providers (with siblings attending a support group). Nine families out of 41 families (22%) indicated that they had little or no regular contact (less than three monthly) with professional workers (Burke 2004, p.61). This contrasts with 9 out of 56 (16%) in the second study. It would appear that although the majority of families are in touch with professional workers (in health, social care or teaching), a significant minority do not maintain regular contact with their key worker. This leaves the families to manage alone, raising the possibility that services were not accessed and, equally importantly, that the needs of siblings were more likely to be further down any list of identified family needs.

It is clear from the two surveys that a relatively high proportion of families with disabled children and siblings do not receive regular professional support. This lack of service provision represents structural stigma, being a failure to identify the needs of siblings when need is probably viewed as the precursor of the disabled child. Some siblings appear to be excluded in the professional considerations of a number of workers.

Case examples

The following two case examples include one drawn from my earlier research (Burke and Cigno 2000). The early case is re-examined and considers how associative conditions help provide a more detailed understanding of the social interactions that are described. The second case was identified after an interview with the family during the second sibling study (Burke and Fell 2007) although not previously published. These cases complement those examined in Burke (2004, p.33), signifying some consistency for the concept of disability by association.

The case of Kelsey and David

Kelsey is aged 13, and has a brother David, aged ten, who was born with cerebral palsy. David is also intellectually impaired, has little speech and walks with difficulty. Until recently, Kelsey and David played happily together and Kelsey enjoyed helping her brother. However, it was when Kelsey started to bring her school friends home that she noticed they treated David differently and that they also seemed frightened of him. One of Kelsey's girlfriends refused to go into the paddling pool because David had been in the pool before her. The family had not considered the impact of such an incident until, during an interview for this research, the question was asked, 'Were the other children a bit frightened of David?' The family had not foreseen the possibility due to their own acceptance of their son.

Comment

David, although included in family events, clearly experienced a form of stigmatisation due to his disability when Kelsey had her friends around. Kelsey had to try to understand why her friends would not enter the pool previously used by David. Perhaps they thought David contaminated the pool in some way, but whatever the cause, an element of anxiety was evident. Kelsey's mother did not know how to help her, only to reassure her that she did not have the 'burden of responsibility' for David; that is, it is not your fault. This did not deal with the fact that Kelsey realised her brother was being treated differently, and in doing so identified an element of difference in her own situation. This was only resolvable by excluding her brother from the possibility of being involved with her friends. Kelsey's experience encouraged her to deny her sibling relationship (not her burden) and so avoid 'disability through association' as the sister of an apparently 'less acceptable' brother. This is stigma of a social kind such that an associative experience spoils Kelsey's identity.

Locus of control. In this case, Kelsey and David appear to have a happy relationship, but parental reactions to Kelsey's friends have led to David being excluded from certain situations. The lack of social acceptance acts as an external control on the family as they adapt to the needs of Kelsey's friends. They do not allow David to play in the pool so that Kelsey does not face a possible rejection from her friends.

The case of Ian and Tom

The family of Ian (12) and Tom (15) were interviewed after completing a questionnaire from the second sibling study. Ian attends mainstream school. His older brother has learning difficulties, little speech and coordination problems. The family realised something was different with Tom during his second year when he was not reaching the usual milestones in walking and talking, which combined with a general lack of responsiveness in play activities led them to realise that he was not developing as might be expected. Ian, subsequently, had no apparent developmental difficulties and soon became the focus of family admiration. Ian is bright and lively, and from discussions it seems he is considered everything that Tom is not.

Comment

In this family, it appears that the tendency for parents to spend more time with their disabled child has been reversed. There is more attention and praise for the non-disabled younger child, who is viewed positively as an all-round achiever. Ian likes sports, and plays football; his brother does not and has problems even kicking a ball. Ian is doing well at school, in contrast with Tom who cannot read or write. However, it is Ian who gets angry when he does not get what he wants, whereas Tom is relatively quiet and introverted, 'living in his own world' according to the parents.

Ian said that his brother can be an 'embarrassment, because people just think he is thick'. Although Ian says he does sometimes have to look after him when he gets home from special school (by school transport), generally they seem to have little to do with each other. This case is one where a sibling has a negative regard for his brother, who is tolerated rather than accepted. Ian's determination to lead his life independently of his brother suggests that he finds Tom socially stigmatising, and this is inadvertently reinforced by the apparent grateful acknowledgement from his family that he is the achiever Tom never will be.

It appears that the family effectively exclude Tom in order to direct their attentions to Ian, who, as a consciously aware child, has developed a negative regard for his brother. This discriminates against the disabled child, who is clearly experiencing a form of social stigmatisation partly constructed by the family, in their attempt to protect Ian and themselves from a disabled identity. It is like a familial fear of disability by association, in the internal family expression centred on Tom's identity that inherently reinforces negative attitudes towards disability. Ian is experiencing disability by association reflected by his difficulty and anger in accepting his sibling's disability. This, it appears, is largely due to the parents emphasising the differences between the two boys.

Locus of control. The question arises as to where the decision-making power rests in this family. It does appear that Ian has the internal control because he is held up as an ideal to some extent by his grateful parents and Tom has learned to be a passive recipient of this hierarchy. Re-thinking the power relationships in this family might give Tom more influence in the family decision-making forum, which would mean enabling him to make choices, even if initially at a basic level.

Discussion
Living with a child with a disability causes reactions, whether indicating the need for a better social life, fewer restrictions at home or concerns about the 'inheritance' factor of disability. Even within families themselves, the social element of stigmatisation is evident, reflected in family dynamics and social interactions. This reinforces the resultant pressures experienced elsewhere, especially when siblings do not appear to do similar things to their peer group.

This all points toward a pessimistic view of disability in the family and is indicative that support should be provided for the families to help resolve conflicting pressures. Parents need to talk to their children about future plans for their disabled child, so that siblings feel included and understand parental intentions rather than living in a state of uncertainty, not being fully aware or necessarily resolving their feelings of responsibility toward their disabled sibling. A sibling support group (Burke 2004; Naylor and Prescott 2004) would probably benefit many siblings, reducing a sense of isolation and difference compared with others while enabling a sharing of experiences with other siblings to achieve a greater sense of acceptance and understanding of disability.

It may be that disability is constructed as a form of normality within the family (Stalker and Connors 2004), but the impact on families socially may create a form of disadvantage for siblings (as with Kelsey cited above). An acceptance of a child's disability should also awaken the need to attend to the non-disabled child whose experience of disability is a formative event in relationships and interactions with peers. One child should not be discriminated against in favour of another, as appears to be the case with Tom. Professional alertness to these matters should provide a focus on the needs of the disabled child *and* siblings, viewing the family holistically.

Conclusion
In drawing together the results from these two sibling studies, conducted in different geographical locations, it is apparent that living as a family with a disabled child inevitably has consequences for the family members. This is probably a self-evident truth, for it would be hard to conceive of any relationships without consequences, but it is because of the need to investigate our understanding of the consequences for siblings that this research was conducted.

What is clear from this research is that living with disability in the family confers a new type of identity in non-disabled siblings, a 'disabled identity', which is referred to as 'disability by association'. The processes that construct disability by association link with social, situational and structural aspects of stigmatisation and are experienced in day-to-day familial and social activities. The focus here has mainly concerned social situations and interactions within the family, although situational and structural elements will be at work, at home, at school and in formal settings relating to welfare services; but this needs further examination to observe interactive experiences beyond the family unit.

The evidence of difference in disability by association is voiced through expressions of regret in living with disability but more often occurs in tandem with positive views of increased maturity in siblings, as reported in this chapter. Restrictions in social life include finding it difficult to do things together as a family, and missed opportunities otherwise available to children in non-disabled families: going on holiday, days out, or having the freedom to bring friends home without the fear of discrimination or prejudice.

The process of helping siblings has been mentioned, through a sibling support group that helps raise self-esteem (Burke 2005; Naylor and Prescott 2004), via counselling and parental recognition (Powell and Gallagher 1993), and through service involvement (Burke 2004). This needs the cooperation of the young people concerned if it is to work. The need for siblings to express their concerns seems vital, although this is not easy to accomplish especially if creating an identity that attempts to fit normality despite the fact of difference, potentially denying the realities of experience. However, to make progress, recognising disability by association helps with an understanding that stigmatisation causes a discriminatory effect that may result in social exclusion.

The positive may often balance the negatives and there are many positives, in families strengthened by a united front, a greater awareness of others, with most siblings sensitive to the needs of their parents and disabled brother or sister. The cases examined suggest reaction by siblings with an associative identity located in their experiences of living with a disabled brother or sister. Disability by association is real; it is about how others treat young people with disabled brothers and sisters, and it is why specific social care provision is needed for them.

Practice notes

Does living with a child with a disability make any difference to a sibling?
The evidence provided in the case examples in this chapter is intended to show that disability does impact on siblings. Siblings not only help care for their disabled brothers or sisters, sometimes referred to as 'young carers', but they may also experience some form of social reaction as a result of the familial association.

Is living with disability restricting?
Living and caring for disabled children will place some restrictions on families, and they have to plan more carefully, organising their lives to do things that are more routine for others. Caring for a disabled child may

entail providing help with basic hygiene, dressing, feeding and toileting, as well as carrying out a supervisory responsibility that may extend beyond the usual age range when many young people become more self-sufficient. A child with behaviour problems, for example, will need supervision, while a child in a wheelchair may require special transportation and access facilities to buildings.

What do we mean by shared care?
Living with disabilities often means that caring is a family concern, involving not only mothers, fathers and siblings, but may include extended family members too. Shared care may also mean sharing care with paid professionals who assist families.

Is service delivery the same as support?
The term 'service delivery' refers to the provision of services of a practical nature. Often this applies to aids but may include access to special activity groups, sitter and respite care services. The family and child will be supported by service provision, but 'support' is often used to mean emotional or therapeutic support which is distinct from services that offer physical resources.

Chapter 7

Listening to Children
with Special Needs

The aim of this chapter is to explain how it is possible to represent the views of children with special needs in terms of their future social and personal development. Professionals know that young people with special needs can often be helped by involving them in varying types of activities that enable them to express their views and opinions. Examples are provided of the group activities followed to enable this process.

This chapter shows that seeking the opinions of young people, whether verbally or non-verbally, promotes a sense of wellbeing and marks the beginning of self-advocacy skills. It is apparent, also, that professionals need to take time to listen to young people, to ascertain their views independently of activities that occur in groups. Young people need to express opinions (not necessarily verbally), individually and collectively. Professionals should ensure that one-to-one opportunities are made available and that views are sought and acted upon.

A number of young people from Yorkshire and London were consulted about their opinions to inform this chapter; see the Appendix (study four) for the design employed. The views expressed by these young people showed that participating in various activities increased their self-confidence and advocacy skills, which led to a more considered expression concerning their perceived collective and individual needs. Talking, and indeed other forms of communication, does help young people to develop opinions.

Special needs
The children in this study had 'special educational needs' identified following a Statement as required within the Education Act 1996. In

defining 'special educational needs', the *Code of Practice* (DfES 2001, 1.3) clarifies need, or learning difficulty, in comparison with the majority of children of the same age. The *Code of Practice* is a guide to the statutory assessment process that is followed before a Statement is issued. An emphasis within any such Statement is the need to listen to children concerning their own unique knowledge of their needs (DfES 2001, 3.2) and so concurs with the United Nations Convention considered in Chapter 2.

Despite the legal entitlement of being heard, as a right of expression, the work of Morris (2001) indicates that children with high levels of support needs experience barriers in accessing services and resources. Indeed, Beresford (1995) found that families with disabled children have limited resources available to them. There are difficulties in defining what is essential when considering the question of 'what is right?' against 'what is available?'

It is evidently pertinent to children's future that, when an experience will make a difference to them, they must be consulted and any action that follows has to incorporate their preferences (DfES 2006; Franklin and Sloper 2007). Earlier research of Burke and Cigno (2001) and Burke and Montgomery (2003) also supports the view that, within a children's rights framework, they need to be listened to and treated as independent individuals with rights of their own, not subsumed by those of their parents or indeed those of professionals. It is a view reinforced by the young people themselves as reported in this chapter.

Independence and autonomy

The children's groups examined were established to encourage independence and autonomy within children who were involved in the groups. Autonomy is described by Dowling (2000, p.83) as 'the degree of freedom which the adult provides to allow the child to experiment, make judgements, choose activities, and express ideas'.

The capacity to make choices is associated with a person's level of confidence, which in turn often depends on a positive sense of self. Self-esteem can change according to the situations experienced. To achieve a degree of autonomy it is necessary to build positive images about oneself. The way in which positive images may be built can rest with the professional social worker whose power should not be underestimated, especially as far as young people are concerned (Farnfield 1998, p.66). This means that the professional worker can actively influence the life of the young person and help him or her to achieve a move from absolute dependence to relative dependence – see Trevithick (2000, p.42) on Winnicott (1975). However, despite the fact that young people may perceive social workers as powerful, it does not follow that a young person will trust the worker. Building trust is therefore an important element in the communication process between the social worker and child.

Group processes help build trust by encouraging an identity for group members with a group facilitator to enable the group to focus on joint activities. The individual worker can in a similar way engage with a young person, verbally, in pen and paper activities, meeting parents and child at the same time, expressing the desire to help and assist, giving positive regard to the young person; all designed to improve the process of communication. The advantage of engaging in an activity – drawing a picture of family members (for example) – is that communication should necessarily involve some object requiring choice, for without choice the building of bridges toward independence can never be made. In the development of self-advocacy skills, Goodley (2005) considers the importance of friendship pairs (between young people of similar ages or interests), which include plans to meet up and make arrangements for outings, etc., as elements for making choices and acting upon them. Thus it seems quite conceivable for the professional to encourage friendship pairing to help achieve a similar objective, while recognising that not all young people (many used to a degree of social exclusion) will happily drop into a group activity, such that an alternative route to choice and independence might be required.

The role of group activities, which inform one-to-one practice, can be elucidated by an examination of the group experiences observed within the following study. The practitioner will see that commitment, including frequent meetings, provides the opportunities which identify whether making choices has the desired effect.

The groups

The Yorkshire group met once a month and if members were not present they were either sent letters or emailed to let them know the date and time of the next meeting. Sometimes the group met in the evenings, in which case the meeting would last for two to three hours. When they met on Saturdays the group took more time, and once (when working on a video of the group) activities started at 11 am and did not finish until

6 pm. The Yorkshire group provided transport when needed; otherwise, group members could make their own arrangements.

The London group first met in a restaurant, known by the young people for its quality chicken and chips. The first meeting was open and followed a circulation of flyers and leaflets to young people with prior involvement with a welfare agency. The group facilitator was instrumental in organising this social function as a project designed to encourage young people with special needs to work together.

In both groups the important lesson to learn is keeping young people informed about a meeting that is to take place. It is a simple device to show commitment, provided the meeting does take place!

Parental involvement

The way a child develops will usually involve parents or carers and no parent or carer will offer exactly the same care or opportunities for their child. Dowling (2000) makes reference to the Commission for Racial Equality's view that there is not a 'best' way to bring up a child because the differences in child rearing practices are as varied within 'White' as among 'Black' families. The relevance of this, as Phillips (1998) points out, is that children may experience stigmatisation because they are seen as different whether by virtue of race, gender or disability. Important, too, is the fact that a number of young people with special needs may have communication difficulties, placing a responsibility on carers, mostly parents, to represent the views of the young people, at a time when views from the latter might not be sought or even considered (Burke and Cigno 2001).

The work represented here, although inclusive of parental views, also reflects the views expressed by the young people themselves. It is a relevant point that young people with special needs will express their views and opinions. This willingness is partly a reflection of group activities, but it is also indicative of the readiness of these young people to talk about themselves. This is a message for professionals: providing the space for discussion promotes the expression of ideas and opinions, which has the potential to bridge the gap between dependence and independence – the essence of self-advocacy.

Data

The Yorkshire group included a range of young people with special needs (see Table 7.1). These were reported by parents as representing learning difficulties ($n = 7$; 23.3%), dyslexia ($n = 6$; 20%), special needs with speech and language difficulties ($n = 5$; 16.6%) and autism or tendencies ($n = 4$; 13.3%). All five of the young people in the London group had 'special needs' but these were not subject to further differentiation. The young people in both groups had needs for educational support beyond that usually provided in mainstream education (hence referral to a support group) and as such had difficulties in coping in a traditional learning environment.

Table 7.1 Special needs in the Yorkshire group

Special need identified	Number of children involved	Percentage
Learning difficulties	7	23.3
Dyslexia	6	20.0
Speech/language difficulties	5	16.6
Autistic/tendencies	4	13.3
Dyspraxia	3	10.0
Other	3	10.0
Poor fine motor skills	2	6.6
Totals	30	99.8*

*Due to rounding.

Three meetings of the Yorkshire group were attended (in addition to individual family interviews) during the field stage of the research, one of which was a feedback meeting following an activity-based weekend. The London-based group involved meeting the five young people concerned; again permissions were sought before the interviews progressed. The experience of attendance at two independent groups left very positive impressions of the gains experienced and expressed by the young people themselves.

The Yorkshire group
Experiences prior to group attendance
Prior to their involvement with the children's group, most young people encountered difficult experiences. For example, the reason for attending the group was summarised by John (13) as follows:

> I started going [to the Yorkshire group] when I was struggling with my work. We got a letter inviting us to go. I thought it would be really boring, but when I went it wasn't. We talked about bullying and how to stop it.

Paul (13) expressed his needs thus:

> I think these problems came from the past. I don't think that I was born with it [dyslexia]. I was doing really bad at school. I had to cooperate with the help I was offered to try and help myself.

A number of those interviewed had consistently received negative criticism at school. For instance, Jonathan said he was always described as lazy; Paul (above) was told that he was 'thick'; Alan's parents were told that the school could do nothing for him; and Sean was initially punished and then excluded from school.

Alan (14) identified the strength and relevance of the group to him by talking about the increasing incidence of vandalism that occurred within his home area:

> They have special needs too, but their parents don't care. They are 'left to rot', they go around trashing everything.

The implication from the above is clear. If Alan had not had the opportunity to attend the group, he too could have been in the position of 'trashing everything', but he now has a secure identity, he belonged to the group and enjoyed the activities: he could see that certain behaviours were not desirable. His level of maturity and self-understanding had grown once his needs had been recognised by others within the group setting. It is apparent that experiencing negative criticism devalues young people, and clearly being involved in joint activities improves their self-regard.

The making of a video
An example of a constructive experience is represented in the making of a video (a major project led by a facilitator – described below) which,

enabled a number of these young people to identify skills and use technical equipment in the production process.

The making of the video channelled certain talents and abilities and became a means through which the young people were able to offer opinions (with the researchers), sometimes unaware that they were doing so and probably due to the concentration on the practical tasks in hand. This project, identified by the facilitator and agreed by group members, helped the group identity owing to sharing of tasks in the creation of the video. Making a video of everyday events and offering a commentary was an activity that was enjoyed by all, as these young people explained:

> We started making a video about how to make it better [for people with special educational needs]. I could be a film director. (Michael, 8)

> I just liked doing stuff like drawing, meeting people and talking to the video camera. It's great. (Sarah, 14)

> You don't have to explain all the time what you need, how you feel, that's a relief. It's a pleasure to come here and make a video to say what it's like to have a disability, to make choices for yourself. (Dean, 16)

The facilitators asked reporters from local newspapers to visit the group on a regular basis and as a result occasional articles would appear in the local press. The group, jointly with another organisation, also produced a magazine in which the young people were featured – this drew very positive responses, as members felt all the more important for the attention received. The key to success here lay in being consulted and having ideas valued.

Activity weekend

The undoubted highlight of the Yorkshire group was attendance at a weekend activity centre in the Lake District, arranged by group organisers with parental permission. Attendance was open to family members and young people from the group. Again activities encouraged comments from these young people, including the following:

> I get to go along because of my brother, he uses a wheelchair now, and he can't walk. My mum and dad came too, to help. We did everything together, archery, exploring, bike riding, all sorts. It was great fun. (Sibling John, 13, who also attended the special needs group)

> It was great being there. I want to go again next time because I made new friends. (Rebecca, 12)

The weekend provided an opportunity to get away from the usual routines with a group of friends who knew each other. It encouraged family participation, and the activities that followed cemented relationships. Going away together encouraged a sense of belonging, vital ingredients for young people previously on the edge of exclusion. This may not necessarily be within the remit of the professional worker in one-to-one situations, but it does demonstrate that family activities, like holidays, can help to unite members. However, holidays can also have the opposite effect, if not carefully planned and if relationships are strained to begin with, and assuming funding is not a problem. Professionals may have within their agencies access to inclusive holiday schemes, and should seek these out for families where such experiences might otherwise not be forthcoming.

Debriefing and empowerment

Families who participated in the activity weekend were invited to a special meeting to evaluate the activities followed. At the meeting, the children and young people evaluated the weekend through group discussion, by drawings and in the use of symbolic figures. For example, in the latter, sunshine cutouts were used to indicate happiness or a rain and cloud cutout to show displeasure. The sunshine symbols were highly evident! Thus, these young people had the chance to practise skills of evaluating, making choices and expressing their opinions; all events encouraged a personal view and made communication about their feelings and choices possible.

The use of symbols should not be underestimated as a means of communication, especially for those with restricted communication abilities. It provides a very clear expression of understanding and meaning. This particular technique works in one-to-one situations, if a professional takes a lead in working with a young person, but it requires an event to be evaluated and reflected upon. Such engagements build up expressive skills, and what one can learn here is that group activities can be incorporated within the professional interview. Clearly debriefing is a process of importance, and might follow any family engagement or activity.

The London group

The London group initially had a core membership of eight young people, and five continuing members were interviewed for this study (nearly 18 months after the group began). Ali, now 18 years old and at college, expressed the intent of the initial meeting:

> We went on about getting a voice because we weren't able to express ourselves in the usual youth clubs or other services. This was our big chance to share our views with people who understood and could listen.

Christa (18) described how she benefited from the group:

> It gives us the chance to say how we feel and what we feel. Everywhere else they don't give you the chance to speak. Here you have the chance.

Within the group, Jennifer (14) said:

> In school the other kids are not so friendly; in this group they understand me. It made me more independent. I never used to go out a lot because of my physical disability, but now I go out mostly on my own. I'm not a stay-at-home person anymore.

James (15) explained that he did not talk until he was six years old:

> The group helped me to talk: it helped my friendship difficulties: it helped my learning difficulties: it helped me to feel better about myself. It's given me a huge confidence boost and the experience of new things. I'm more assertive.

This is a considerable development from the beginning when the expectation was that relationships might develop. This represents a challenge which would have been inconceivable for these group participants before they joined and felt they belonged within this group. Evidently these young people have developed interpersonal skills, especially in being able to express their views to a complete stranger (to them), the interviewer, available for a relatively short time only.

Common experiences within the special need groups

The group environment in general provided outlets through which the group members could exercise opinions, make judgements and choices, and take responsibility for themselves. Through some of the group activities, like the making of the video, the young people in both groups were able to establish a collective voice. However, of the children and young people interviewed, some did not regularly attend sessions provided and some had stopped going altogether. Six young people from the 15 families interviewed in the Yorkshire group attended intermittently. Paul

(18) and Jonathan (15) went along occasionally out of a sense of responsibility for the younger group members. They, as the oldest members of
the Yorkshire group, were the most critical of it:

> I think I'd have got more out of the group if I'd gone when I was
> younger... I think it's running fine for them [the younger children] but
> it's not targeted for people my age.

What this demonstrates is that peer identification is important. In the
London group the members were that bit older, so they had a stronger
group identity based on shared age-related activities and discussion.
However, when the age range was more exclusively for a younger age
group, as it seemed to Paul and Jonathan, then they felt a little out of
place, but felt duty bound to continue their involvement, acting more
like mentors for the younger members than, necessarily, having their
own perceived needs met.

It is apparent that young people liked an identity with a group of
young people with similar previous experiences and difficulties within
the education system. This view followed earlier negative experiences at
school, before finding that joint group activities in a group of young
people who understood these difficulties was not restrictive and
promoted the sharing of opinions. Many had reported that had not felt
they 'belonged' in their experience at school, possibly due to the perceived stigma of having 'special educational needs' or somehow being
viewed as different owing to some perceived disability. The overwhelming message is that group membership is beneficial and appears to
improve the sense of self-esteem and wellbeing for these young people.
This is part of the move to self-advocacy, the capacity to represent one's
self. Membership of groups should be a transferable concept to family
situations when the professional worker or facilitator helps young
people with special needs to be more actively regarded within the family.
Clearly, activity-based experiences can be reflected upon and views
sought, and so represent developmental opportunities for the young
people involved.

Self-advocacy
The needs of people with learning disabilities, contextualised here as
'special needs', are underpinned in the *Valuing People* document (DoH
2000b), where involving those whose needs are to be addressed is an
important policy imperative. However, while such intents are laudable as

a result of a policy directive, putting policy into practice may fall on stony ground if those consulted are incapacitated by a lifestyle and experiences which previously failed to seek or under-represented their opinion. Clearly improving self-advocacy skills can begin to be achieved only when involving people with special needs in matters which concern them becomes everyday practice; this is neither tokenistic nor paternalistic. Self-advocacy builds on the ability to express feelings, to represent oneself, but it cannot work if no one listens.

Consequently, professionals, as a starting point, need to listen. This is not an amazing fact, yet its importance can be underestimated if listening involves listening only to carers or representatives and not to the individual whose needs are central to the debate. There are difficulties in incorporating the views of those who cannot communicate through the usual means or channels, as Fitton (1994) explains – but understanding can come via gestures and signals that can be used to indicate an accord or disagreement with a given proposal or view. The danger is that, as earlier research has shown (Burke and Cigno 1996), for young people with learning disabilities the wishes of verbally able parents might express views counter to those of the offspring. The need is for a beginning partnership between professionals and the young person who, in this context, has special needs. This should not, and cannot legally, exclude parents; but it is a necessary step if a young person is to be heard. It leads to self-advocacy as a means for representation of one's own views which may differ from those of others.

Discussion and considerations for the future

This special needs study reports the views expressed by young people attending an independent educational advisory group in Yorkshire and is compared with views from young people attending a similar group in London. Significant issues were raised by the ethics of undertaking work with young people and these were reviewed (see Chapter 2 and Appendix). The young people involved in the research reported their self-confidence and advocacy skills improved due to their group experience. In both groups, members were committed to participation in project-based activities that raised their self-esteem and helped establish a sense of their own identity and purpose.

Fifteen children in two groups were interviewed for this study (together with 35 parents). The group members expressed similarities in the way group experiences impacted on them. It appears that children identified as having 'special needs' do benefit from attending a children's group. In both group settings, the opportunity for developing an independent view was fostered among the children involved and this was apparent in the children's descriptions of their group experiences.

The experience of social exclusion, particularly in the sense of isolation reported, and as typified by the two groups considered, is remedied in part by inclusion within another setting. Developing opinions and views among the young people themselves, whilst supporting the growth of a framework that recognises each child's needs and responsibilities independent of their parents, seemed invaluable (Fortin 2003, p.59). Although the needs of the family remain of equal importance, individual needs are not necessarily the same as those of other family members. The simple device of providing an opportunity for acceptance has enabled the young people involved to feel that they belong.

It was proposed earlier that children across the ethnic, cultural and class backgrounds do not necessarily have the same needs (Phillips 1998). Given the small sample size of this study some questions remain about whether a common identity is established simply on the grounds of other people's assessment of special needs or whether there is also a need to respond creatively along different lines of personal identity. However, this study has shown that the Yorkshire and the London groups reported similar positive benefits. The London group was more diverse in class and ethnic group representation. Despite this, and with leadership and support, a group identity and membership was forged and sustained. Indeed the issue of age as being vital is again implicated in that the sense of purpose reflected in the interviews with London group members was very high indeed.

It would appear that a number of factors contribute to the success of groups for children with special needs. Fundamental to the group experience was 'getting away', whether from school, from home, or from settings where they felt less accepted. In both settings, a sympathetic understanding of each young person's needs, views and wishes is apparent. To be able to let these shine through represents an important quality for any group leader who facilitates activities based on shared involvement and choices made with the young people themselves. The need is for facilitation with gentle direction and encouragement.

Practice notes

What are special needs?

This term is used collectively to describe the situation of children and young people who have a variable range of intellectual or physical incapacity. A child with special needs will be the subject of a Statement of Special Needs under the legislation, which then prescribes how those needs should be met. Special needs, as an educational assessment within a Statement, is designed to help identified children make the best of their educational opportunities. In some ways special needs might be considered a bridge between a disability (as a social construct) and an impairment (as a medically defined condition).

Why interview young people with special needs?

Talking to young people is important to see if they have views to offer. The interviews represented in this chapter were often aided by having a focus for the discussion, an activity being followed at the time of the meeting (e.g. making a video). Communication was aided in the activity weekend debriefing using symbols on cards which helped the less verbally able young people to show and express their views. Interviews were, nevertheless, limited in scope and range of discussion, due in part to research difficulties (not having a sufficient range of communication methods), but are important when demonstrating an interest in the young people and can only be a beginning in recognising the need for communication between professionals and the young people they are expected to understand. The results show that these young people have opinions and can make choices which have to be considered in professional decision-making.

Is the parental role any different due to caring for a disabled child?

In the context of this chapter the parental role relates to their input into the care needs of the disabled child. Essentially the parental role is not different from that of any other parent in caring for offspring; however, one should never underestimate the many adjustments that living with disability places on parents, who may view their task as an everlasting responsibility without any expectation of independence for their child. For example, a child of 15 years may be near to independence during the latter school stages but a child with disabilities may still need care and supervision. A severely disabled child of 15 may still have to be spoon-fed, such that parental responsibilities may become locked into the need of a much younger child who is, in every other respect, a young adult. (See also practice notes in Chapter 9 on achieving independence.)

Acknowledgement

This chapter uses data which the author initially reported in the *Journal of Learning Disability* (Burke 2005).

Chapter 8

Support Groups for Children and Young People

This chapter examines the recurring features that exist within a number of apparently successful support groups that were set up to help either young people with special needs or their siblings. An earlier finding was that group attendance enables individuals to begin to identify with group members, creating a club type of identity, which helps build a sense of self-worth (Burke 2005). The intent here is to show that a need exists to extend professional responsibility beyond the individual one-to-one approach and to demonstrate that utilising group processes produces an additional means for helping service users. This chapter shows how these groups work and draws lessons that may be applied in practice.

The broad features of the groups reported in this chapter should clarify and inform professionals of the benefits of group experiences in raising the social status of group members. To achieve this aim it is probably a good idea to ask whether the young people involved thought the group attendance was worthwhile, and this is the starting point for the chapter. The chapter will conclude with a summary of the main areas identified for good practice.

The research evidence on group activities, particularly Dies (1992), suggests that there is little difference in the success rates between individual and group treatment. However, Riva and Kalodner (1997) indicate that the expertise and knowledge gained from group research should inform practice. The latter point was informed by Bednar and Kaul (1994), who following an extended period of research into groups, concluded that clients benefited in a variety of ways. Groups should aim to counteract the effect of negative experiences which, as Dowling (2000, p.11) explained, 'are inevitably going to leave children feeling inadequate…that they have failed'. Clearly, if group processes work, then professionals should encourage young people who might benefit to take advantage of any opportunities made available.

Some of the evidence
Opinions of the sibling support group
The response from 41 families whose children attended the siblings group evaluated in the second study (see Appendix) was overwhelmingly favourable. Of the 38 who completed the evaluation question on the usefulness of the sibling group meetings, 33 families rated the group as very helpful and five as fairly helpful. The responses from siblings themselves echo this finding; in particular, the opportunity to meet on a regular basis was generally welcomed as an enjoyable experience, confirming the trend identified in the pilot study (Burke and Montgomery 2000). Comments by siblings illustrate their feelings and mixed emotions:

> It's easier to talk about your sibling with people who know what it is like. (12-year-old girl)

> She's like Jekyll and Hyde, pulling things about and throwing them. She'll break anything left about, but she has big smiles and is really loving and kind. (13-year-old girl)

> The more I play with her the less she bugs me. (14-year-old boy)

Clearly, this is indicative of free exchanges among group members, engendering a sense of group identity in a safe environment.

Opinions of the special needs group
This group (see Appendix) gave weight to the opinions of the children to reinforce individual contributions. This showed young people that they were valuable, a factor likely to raise levels of self-confidence and encourage some degree of autonomy. The comments of group members reflect their experience of the group:

> It gave me a chance to socialise and talk to friends. I liked drawing the 'paper people'. I like watching the video. I like the way it is. (15-year-old girl)

I'm the sort of person who likes to tell other people about my opinions now. I have lots of friends. It's nice to be in this group. (12-year-old boy)

It's nice going there to talk to people, it makes me feel better afterwards. (14-year-old girl)

People go to learn more and to give their opinions. (12-year-old girl)

I like doing things I've not done before. I like meeting new friends. (10-year-old boy)

These young people had, prior to attending the group, felt some degree of exclusion from mainstream activities. Despite this negative early experience, the group was capable of a consistent level of enthusiasm and interest in organised activities.

Young people going to the group related to each other in a different way from when at school and in other social situations. According to her mother, Sarah (10) talked about problems and difficulties to the other children in the group in a way that she did not at school. Paul (14) expressed his experience as follows: 'I have a lot of friends without problems; sometimes it's nice to hear other people, like, who know that sort of stuff.'

This indicates that the group experience enabled a sharing of problems and difficulties away from the everyday situation at school, where it might not be possible to express or share fears and anxieties. The children's group provided a happy, supportive and developing experience, and the activity weekend featured as the main pursuit to which group members expected to attend, and was reflected upon as a consolidating group experience.

Induction stress

Membership of a group was not always easily achieved. The initial stages of joining a group were stressful, characterised according to Corey (2004, p.90) by a sense of 'anxiety and insecurity'. However, through talking about their disabled brothers and sisters in a structured way and through sharing experiences they realised they were not completely alone in their experiences after all, and initial anxieties were overcome. Prior to joining a sibling support group children often said that they felt a sense of isolation due to the differences, compared with their school friends, of having a disabled brother or sister. However, through becoming part of the group most found that this sense of isolation reduced.

For example, Jenny (15) said of the group sessions: 'Helped you to realise you're not the only one; other people have brothers and sisters like you.' For Matthew (15), talking about his feelings was an all-important activity. Group sessions enabled the exchange of ideas and issues, such as mixed feelings about having a disabled brother and sister, or in being bullied at school, which could be shared with others who understood.

Common understanding

Not everybody wanted to talk about their family experiences. For these children, being around others who understood how they felt, *without explanations*, was a very positive aspect of being in the group. Sarah (13) commented: 'You don't have to talk about it; they [other group members] know how you feel. However, talking about it *is* important, and Dean (16) from the special needs group was able to express some negative feeling he harboured about his school experiences:

> I go to a mainstream school. They say they treat me the same as everyone else, but when I need the loo, I have to ask for help. Now they tell me that I need two helpers because I'm 'vulnerable'. Who do they think they are protecting, surely it is my choice how and who should help me.

Although Dean was justifiably angry at the treatment he received from his otherwise helpful school, he felt the school's understanding of his needs were superficial and only in the support group could he express his true feelings. His 'vulnerability' at school was due to the fact that he did not and could not deal with the intrusion into his most private functioning, and so he restrained his visits to the toilet (coping with the discomfort) until he returned home.

Listening to other young people and becoming aware that they share both common experiences and feelings seems to result in a close bond between them, and friendships take on a new importance. Sometimes friendships formed continue beyond the duration of the group sessions, but even when they did not, the experiences were still considered valuable. When in the group the impediments to friendships, which existed for them elsewhere, no longer apply. 'Disabled' is accepted and is not present in a way that makes these young people feel different from their peers as they do at school. One teenage male sibling expressed this view: 'People pick on my sister, and make me feel bad, but this does not happen in the siblings group.'

Several members of the sibling group nearly all enjoyed the activities, though not all of them could remember more than one activity. Matthew (9) enjoyed 'running around and playing and making things, it's fun'. Art was a popular activity across the age range, but not everyone enjoyed all activities. Mark (8) said 'It was OK but I didn't like some of the stuff, like the baking.'

Weekend activities and weeks away were rated more highly than evening sessions. For Nicola (13) a weekend away from her disabled sister gave her a rare opportunity to be herself. The weekend activities were thought to be exciting and offered opportunities not normally expected by children in families with disabled children. According to Holly (13): 'We did all the things I wanted to do, skydiving, motor biking and abseiling. It's brilliant.' Tom (12) was very enthusiastic about the week he had spent on a barge. Some siblings who have not been away with the group expressed the hope that they would have the opportunity to do so in the future – it seemed a high point in sibling group activities. Also, to be asked for an opinion had the potential to raise self-esteem, as the question focused on the individual's view reflecting the expectation to participate and contribute to the group's functioning.

In the special needs group, the comparative element from the London group evaluation produced no negative feedback. All five young people said they found the group helpful in a number of ways. The only change suggested was by James (15): 'I'd like to meet more new people. That would help me make more friends.' This appears to reflect James's potential for development, which clearly group membership had encouraged, to the point where he wanted new experiences beyond the group and appeared to have matured and gained more confidence as a result of the shared group activities.

What should change

The young people interviewed in the second study (the sibling group) and the fourth study (the special needs group) thought that changes to the support group would improve its functioning. These concerned the frequency and length of meetings, the age range of group members and the involvement of parents.

First, group members did not like the long gaps between the available sessions, so membership felt transitional. Interestingly, one boy with special needs expressed a desire more representative of the sibling group view: 'I wish it was more like a regular youth club; you could go every week and meet your mates, not feel it was set up because I've been told I've special needs.'

Second, the age of members within the group concerned a number of young people. Some felt uncomfortable when the age range of the group was too wide. Jenny (15) felt out of place in her group of 10- and 11-year-olds but, nevertheless, liked the group and found the sessions useful. An 18-year-old said: 'I was too old for the group, but I could see it could be fun.' However, an age split also produced some regret for a sibling group member who had a younger sister. Sarah (12) said: 'I've got away from her but I'm missing her.' Generally, age appropriateness seemed important to these young people.

Third, when parents were occasionally involved some of the special needs group felt they were not independent enough of their parental involvement, especially when meeting collectively following the more usual group activities. This contrasted with the siblings group where parents were effectively excluded from group activities. A lack of clarity existed among parents about the organisation of the group sessions themselves. They said that they had little idea about what went on during the group sessions. They understood that it was their children's time for themselves. Perhaps the solution is a balance between these extremes: enough parental contact to reassure both parties, but sufficient distance to enable a degree of independence for the young people.

It is important that the group members enjoyed the sense of physical freedom at group sessions. It is also important that, having provided opportunities for young people to express themselves so that they, in turn, are enabled to be critical of the help they receive, they need to be listened to. Taking account of these views is all-important to the continued functioning of the group.

Parental opinions

As found with the young people themselves, the main source of discontent among parents was the uncertainty of group provision. According to one mother who was in touch with other mothers:

> Mums are distraught that the groups run for such a short time. Then we don't always know when the next group will run. It's a problem with resources, whatever that means.

One parent made the following comment about the siblings group:

> Our son was lucky to attend a sibling's support group at a time when he was questioning why his brother was disabled. The group should be permanent so siblings can 'dip in and out' and have a sounding board where they can share their experiences and not feel alone.

Another made the brief comment:

> The group gave the kids the chance to do things they otherwise could not, things I could not do with the caring we have to do – that's got to be good for them.

It is clear that both the sibling and special needs groups were seen as a valuable provision, but both groups were offered for limited periods or at too low a frequency. As one mother summarised the problem: 'What do they do for the other weeks of the year?' Parents knew, however, that they would receive a letter informing them when the group for their child was due to start, but they had little idea about how long their child would have to wait.

A preference was expressed that the group should meet at least once a month, throughout the whole year. It was generally considered better to have a regular meeting to look forward to than to have the uncertainty of not knowing if and when the next group session might begin.

Parents clearly do like some feedback from the group leaders to ensure that what goes on has their approval, and their perception is that this does not happen in the sibling group. As expressed earlier, the opposite problem existed for the special needs group where parental involvement was more hand-in-hand with the activities of the young people, even to the extent of having a joint weekend away from the home locality. It seems a little unfortunate that the requirement for security within the group should exclude a more proactive approach toward achieving independence. A form of syllabus might attend to this need, perhaps combined with an attendance certificate to indicate the activities with which a particular child had been involved.

Dyson (1996) argues that young people will lose confidence and feel a sense of lowered self-esteem if not included in family discussions to enable their concerns to be aired. Group activities help develop the confidence to discuss concerns and to offer opinions, leading to the prospect of being included in future family discussions. If issues are not resolvable in the group, then the group leader should take some responsibility in reporting back to parents, as tended to happen with the special needs group but not with the siblings group.

Value put on organised activities

For many young people the value of the sibling group was not just in the attending, as the following, gained from interviewing after a group meeting, illustrate.

Philippa (13) is worried about what will happen to her younger disabled sister. She says 'What is wrong with her?' She says she tries to understand her sister's needs, and recognises that the future holds difficulties for her, but finds it difficult to understand her special needs. Holly (13) worries about her brother, 'whether anyone will take him in, marry him and have kids'. Holly is concerned that her brother could not initiate a relationship, set up home and take responsibility for his family, although if he led a more independent life it would remove some of the responsibility she feels for him.

The group sessions enabled discussion of these concerns, not necessarily resolving them, but enabling a sharing with other young people who listened. In the special needs group the sense of group identity was strong, and the increased expression of views helped the young people to understand that they could make choices and influence decisions, and although for most this concerned group activities, it represented a step towards self-determination.

The overwhelmingly positive view of most group members is expressed concerning the activities within the group. 'It's brilliant, it's the best, it's something to look forward to' were typical responses across the age range. Jennifer (14) from the special needs group said: 'The group gives you the chance to talk, and for once, someone will listen to me, that helps you live a bit.'

Whether or not all the plans reached fruition seemed not always to matter, the important thing being able to plan and being able to follow the plan through to some extent. The young people gained experience in exercising their right to make choices and pursue their own decisions, and were able to indicate that their newly acquired skills were valued. Indeed, this seemed exactly in line with the report *Valuing People* (DoH 2001b), which recommends the need for choice and opportunity.

The attention to group activities is what Adams (1996) recognises, when he describes empowerment as a consequence of achieving a degree of self-determination and independence, but it may manifest itself in more subtle ways. Group sessions were used in the special needs group to talk about bullying and included discussion on finding practical solutions to stop it. Such discussions have the potential to equip children to handle situations more effectively, perhaps not achieving the sense of full empowerment as young people, but with a sense of increased self-esteem the move towards self-determination is achieved.

Discussion

It would appear that going along to a group is a liberating experience; it was the best thing that most of the young people involved had done. A lasting feature of the special needs young people was the sense of 'growing up' and an absolute faith and loyalty to the group to which they belonged. Friendship patterns emerged for both groups, which members valued highly. This may be because group members experienced a sense of freedom from the restraints at home that are due to circumstantial restrictions imposed on the family. Both groups enjoyed an atmosphere of common understanding, where no explanations are sought, and peers know how they feel. Essentially these young people gain a voice to express their fears, anxieties and wishes for the future among people who understand, often other young people with needs similar to their own.

The professional role in facilitating such groups is of considerable importance for it enables a positive identity to be gained by young people, once they overcome the initial fear of not belonging and begin to share their feelings with their peers. The vital message is gaining access to a group because the expression of feelings and attitudes is possible: it may not happen at home. The group may not be the only answer because it is successful. In offering a note of caution, some young people will need individual help, and one or two felt very worried about joining a group owing to a perception that they were being classed as different. With such children, professional workers may need to facilitate one-to-one attention, offered as a natural development, not increasing the sense of needing special help – reinforcing, as it were, an increased sense of difference in needing support. It may be that disability for such isolated children is perpetuated by an accumulation of discriminations, as occurs with race, gender and low socioeconomic status – a layering effect that can lead to withdrawal and isolation. Needs can be met, but they have to be identified in the first place. These research studies indicate that the brothers and sisters and disabled siblings all have needs where professional help may begin by encouraging inclusive assessments.

Summary

The data for both siblings and special needs groups provides evidence that the support group experiences that were evaluated were beneficial for those choosing to attend. The group factors that were common to both groups are summarised below:

1. The opportunity for developing an independent view was fostered among the children and this was apparent in the young people's own descriptions of their group experiences. Developing opinions and views, independent of their parents, seemed invaluable.

2. The experience of social exclusion, particularly in the sense of isolation reported, is reduced by attending a group. The simple device of providing an opportunity for acceptance has enabled these young people to feel that they belong.

3. It should be noted that the attention of the group leaders contributed to the level of achievement reached, especially when being open to group suggestions.

4. Fundamental to the group experience was 'getting away', whether from school, from home, or from settings where they felt less accepted.

5. The need is for facilitation with gentle direction, encouragement and respecting of the views of the young people. Group experiences certainly benefited the young people in this study, as highlighted by their reported increase in confidence, in verbal expression and raised self-esteem.

6. Support groups help to raise the profile of young people, and encourage social inclusion.

Valuing People (DoH 2001b), as the title implies, is a key ingredient to success, although the choice here was limited to a particular group membership, suggesting that acceptance must first precede the opportunity offered by diverse group activities.

It appears that support groups help to raise the profile of young people, and encourage social inclusion. This is a requirement for a broader range of disadvantaged children, to include the disabled child and siblings, whose needs might at least be equal or indeed greater than those interviewed and where potential gains might lead to similar levels of success. The term 'success' is a value judgement, although the views expressed by the young people themselves demonstrate that the experiences gained were of substantial benefit to them.

Practice notes

What is a support group?

A support group is designed to help young people with similar experiences (in the context of this chapter, living with a disabled sibling) to deal with aspects of their lives that they might find challenging. This is often achieved by pursuing activities with others with similar needs, all of which is designed to attain a sense of self-worth and achievement when specific tasks are accomplished. Support is enabled by a group facilitator and by sharing and engaging in activities in a non-threatening environment.

What is group provision?

This usually relates to the resources that are made available to meet the needs of group members. It will often be determined according to the funding available to the group facilitators. Group provision may be partly or wholly determined by group members. Self-determination within a group is encouraged by participating in decision-making, which builds up individual self-esteem (see also Chapter 7). However, if resources do not match the requirements of the group then the effect could be counter-productive, when frustration is added into the equation of the vulnerable and needy.

What do we mean by induction stress?

Joining a group for the first time is usually associated with some anxiety owing to uncertainty about how welcome an individual will be made to feel. Induction stress is about being a stranger in a new situation.

Should we inform parents about activities followed within a group?
The wish of parents to know about the nature of activities followed within a group is in potential conflict with the group's ability to be self-determining. Consequently there is a balancing of needs between a parent's right to know and a group's right to confidentiality and self-determination. The latter might be overridden, for example, if a group is determined to undertake potentially dangerous activities like 'hang-gliding' when parental permissions will be required.

Why consider future needs?
It is necessary to consider where one is going. In group situations, the group may restrict membership to certain age groups, or restrict developments to an older age group, such that the continuing needs of newer members may seem to be sidelined. Future needs are about growing up and the preparations required, and group membership should offer a sense of continuity beyond the immediate or early belonging to the group and its activities, as a progressive staging to adulthood.

Chapter 9

A Positive Framework for Empowerment and Inclusion in Social Care

In drawing together the material examined within this book it is apparent that living as a family with a disabled child has consequences for all family members. This is probably a self-evident truth, for it would be hard to conceive of any relationships without consequences; but it was to seek an understanding of the consequences for the family as a whole that these investigations and research into childhood disability were conducted. What is identified is that living with disability confers a form of 'secondary disability' in the non-disabled sibling and other family members, which I refer to as 'disability by association'. Disability by association links to social, situational and structural aspects of stigmatisation in defining the disabled family. It should be reaffirmed here that the intent is not to identify disability as a problem; rather it is to understand how disability is reacted to by the family, including the disabled child, and in relation to others in the wider social setting. This chapter examines the need for professional support across family needs, and within a life spectrum of disability from dependency to independent living.

Caring, social exclusion and practice knowledge

In my earlier research into family support needs (Burke and Cigno 1996), I referred to Dalley (1993). That author suggested that the 'familist ideology' explained why the family is central to offers of support from professionals. This perspective has had a lasting impact on my research because it indicated that the family is at the hub of childhood development in terms of service provision and resource allocation. In the case of the family with a disabled child, the family would for most day-to-day matters tend to its own care needs as it saw them. It was noted that women were usually the primary carers of their disabled children and that siblings take on supportive caring responsibilities, including supervision, being another pair of hands, and acting as chief playmate for the disabled child. This is substantiated by my research which showed that, even with families whose children attend a sibling support group, some families existed in isolation from welfare professionals and other services. This can perpetuate a sense of family isolation, a form of social exclusion, as each family gets on with its own business. But at the same time there is an indication that most families would welcome increased professional contact.

The family with a disabled child is, according to Barr (1999), a disabled family. Siblings recognise this as a fact, even should parents pretend it is not the case. The sense is that disability is often negatively reinforced by contacts with relatives, friends, neighbours and indeed some professionals. Professional interests, as part of a legal requirement, have to centre on 'children in need' or 'special needs children' (an educational perspective), with primary concern for the disabled child. This focus of concern may mean that other family members have their own rights and feelings excluded. Child disability involves all the family; it affects its functioning, its ability to do things together, its perception by others, and indeed, its perception of itself.

Ensuring that each child receives equal care and consideration therefore implies a partnership where parties 'play a key role in promoting a culture of cooperation between parents, schools, LEAs and others' (DfES 2001, 2.1). Social, educational and health professionals will normally take into account both parental and the child's opinion when making recommendations concerning how the 'needs' of a child should be met. Another way with disabled children is to work with them more directly, to provide an enabling environment, such as may exist within group activities. The possible role of such group work is the focus of the investigation reported in Chapter 8.

Support groups are most helpful to siblings who have experienced some denial of their own needs in the past. Indeed, families may create a 'myth' about their own experience, such that siblings experience a form of child neglect, and then professionals will need even greater vigilance to ensure the needs of *all* children within the family are met. Attending a group for children with special needs also provided much support for the young people interviewed, but their identity could be partly subsumed by enthusiastic parents who were keen for a close involvement with the group activities (this being the opposite end of the spectrum to the sibling support group where parental involvement was not encouraged). The solution seemed mid-way: some parental involvement but not to the distraction of the main purpose of the group, which is for the young people themselves.

The issue of individual rights concerns the right to choose, but choice does not exist when there is exclusion by others from activities one wishes to engage in. Exclusion may also relate to an inability to manage if choice is not usually offered. Practitioners might assess the lack of choice as a risk, and so identify the need to compensate for or reduce the risk when providing extra support, and so enable the maintenance of individual choice. Holdsworth (1991) indicates that underpinning her theory, relating to treating people with disabilities equally, is the view that people have the right to make choices. This fits with the right not to be discriminated against and the need to treat individuals positively, clearly described in *Valuing People* (DoH 2004b) where choice and opportunity for people with learning disabilities is advocated.

Professionals, however, may sometimes counter the need for choice depending on the vulnerability of the individual (Burke *et al.* 1997), particularly if a child with disabilities, despite the loving care undertaken by most families, is considered more at risk of neglect and abuse as a vulnerable person (Westcott 1991). A study by Sullivan and Knutson (2000) concluded that children with disabilities are 3.4 times more likely to suffer maltreatment than non-disabled children. A disabled child who is vulnerable is also more at risk if isolated without extended family support, friends, contacts or professional help. The balance that needs to be achieved in working with families where there is a child with a disability is a delicate one; it is sometimes a balance between choice and protection.

The underlying need is to empower the vulnerable. This may be the family if isolated. A professional, if sensing an inability to change, is therefore expected to promote the active involvement of the family and initiate their desire for an improved social standing. This is needed to regain some internal control, including the assertiveness necessary in representing their rights individually and collectively. It is in this context of family experience that the family is associated with disability, as reflected by the experience of siblings documented in Chapter 6.

Disability by association, in its broader representation (Burke and Parker 2007), is a reflection of the stigmatising experience of disempowerment. The evidence of difference is voiced through a range of expressions, from regret at living with disability to positive views of increased maturity, as reported in this text. Experiences of restrictive social life consist of finding it difficult to do things together as a family and missed opportunities otherwise available to children in non-disabled families, whether going on holiday, days out or having the freedom to bring friends home without the fear of discrimination, prejudice or simply an uncertainty in dealing with a child that is different.

I have found from listening to the needs of families, siblings of children with disabilities and children with special needs that the necessity is to find a mechanism to express their views and to voice their feelings concerning their needs, wants and desires. All children, in particular, need the opportunity to speak for themselves, in whatever way they can, and all need to do so to militate against any disadvantage brought about by their home circumstances, background, race, culture or experience. Practitioners should enable that to happen – it is fundamental to the principles of empowerment and individual rights.

Recognising difference

In the earlier part of my research, as reported in this text, the nature of disability and impairment was identified. As the impairment became known to the family, through the timing of diagnosis and the response by family members, most families experienced a sense of relief to know and learn what an impairment actually meant to them. Parents needed to realise that when siblings live in the family they initially know little other than their family experience, so 'difference' for siblings was not, in the early stages of diagnosis, as much an issue for them as it was for their parents. However, according to the social model of disability, it appears that siblings experience a sense of disability by association, as they are perceived by many as different from their friends. Children and young people with special needs also perceive a real difference, in social situations, and both siblings and children with disabilities need support to aid their self-expression.

It is important to emphasise that professionals should recognise the additional stress experienced by the family in caring for a disabled child, compared with families that do not have disabled members, and that this shared experience between parents and siblings is something that increases as the family matures as a 'disabled family unit'. Siblings sometimes take on caring responsibilities for parents, and mothers are often not able to follow previous paid employment because time is at a premium. Practitioners should note that older siblings are more aware of differences between themselves and their brother or sister with a disability particularly when they are expected to take on caring responsibilities, which serve to emphasise the real differences in their respective capabilities and social standing compared with their peers.

Assessment
Bridging the social and medical worlds
Oliver and Sapey (2006) blame a lack of coordination between health and social care professionals as being due to differences in the perceptions of children's needs and a lack of communication between professionals and children themselves. Consequently, we must bridge the medical and social worlds to gain our fullest understanding of needs for the family as a whole.

In social care, professionals may follow an integrated social model and medical model to form a person-centred approach to assessing the needs of the service user. This was identified in Burke (1993) and developed in Burke and Cigno (2000). The working model has similarities to that proposed by Shakespeare (2006) where, in order to understand disability, it is necessary to realise the disabling element of social experience combined with a recognition of an individual's level of impairment. Such a person-specific approach is central to an understanding of the needs of individuals considered disabled. The reality in working with families is that a disabled child is considered to be such owing to some condition, the impairment.

This current research review would suggest that family needs cannot be evaluated soon enough, and the social work profession in particular is guilty of being content to let parents and their children 'go it alone'. That fits with a philosophy based on self-determination and user empowerment, but might well be just an excuse not to get involved. Social work involves taking risks in making assessments: deciding whether the potential benefits of involvement outweigh the drawbacks of exclusion. Practice may, however, be informed by differing perspectives relating to disability in the family – in child care as featured in family work, and in community care in relation to work with adults.

Child care assessment

Assessment in child care is based on children being enabled to have the opportunity to grow and develop within the family. This can be achieved, according to Jackson (2000, p.21), by identifying a means for planning the future wellbeing of the child in offering support and guidance to the family, including short-term or long-term care away for the home if required. Instruments for making assessment have been referred to, including the *Framework for Assessment* (DoH 2000a) which is designed to be used by professionals to provide a common system in identifying child development needs.

Criticisms of the framework (Garrett 2003; Houston 2002; Powell 2001) assert that it is not fully representative of needs when making an assessment. It seems that the framework might be too expansive to have the focus required for a family assessment. This is probably due to the broad-based ecological perspective, when what is really needed is an assessment grounded in family needs, with each family member being identified separately and collectively. The triangular representation of the assessment framework seems to be inadequate for the assessment process (Donald and Jureidini 2004). Assessments require, as identified by Jack (1997), a more systematic framework.

Community care assessment

In community care (which will impact on young people increasingly once reaching the age of 18 years) assessment involves providing a comprehensive picture of user needs and finding the services to meet them (Griggs 2000). The latter means that needs are not equated with services; rather the intent is to define needs first and then to provide services to meet those needs. Hence what is wanted is a needs-led service, rather than a service-led approach which focuses on needs to be met according to available resources.

Given these differing models of assessment it seems pertinent to ask what assessment should strive to achieve. Trevithick (2000, p.61) has identified the purpose of an assessment as helping service users in three ways:

1. Prevent a deterioration by maintaining the quality of life by providing support and help.

2. Introduce limited changes compatible with the needs of the user.

3. Introduce more radical changes where needed but supportive of the individual user.

The purpose of assessment, as Trevithick identified with reference to Trotter (1999, p.116), is sometimes different from points (1) and (2). The need is to introduce a more radical change when service users are resistant to continuing on their life course as it is and lack a sense of hope for the future. The degree of change may be dependent on the user's ability to take on personal responsibility, as discussed by Burke (1998, p.103; 2004, p.30). An *internal locus of control* accepts an individual's ability to take responsibility, and is therefore preferable to an external locus with its associated dependency on others to make decisions. It may also be due to an inherent defence mechanism that denies the reality of the experience of living with a disabled child that a sense of empowerment needs to be engendered within families; such a change would be radical if altering an established pattern of grudging acceptance. By implication, applying the sense of community care within the family perspective, it is possible to relocate the desired focus back within the family in making an assessment of needs.

Practice implications
In practice the capacity to make decisions appears to relate to the order of the decision being taken. So, for example, protective parents may be unable to make a decision (lacking an internal locus of control) to allow their disabled child to enter into independent living arrangements. However, they may accept a sitter or a short-term care solution to provide brief respite from their caring responsibilities. By implication, applying the sense of community care, as an adult provision to a family child care model of assessment, meeting needs may then go some way to bridge the gap by providing resource-based solutions. This relocates the focus on the family's need for assessment, while viewing the disabled child as a developing adult with his or her own needs that have to be included in the assessment process. Such a view may enable protective parents to see that their disabled child has a right to a life of his or her own, as indeed they have themselves.

Locus of control

The social care professional may perceive the locus of control as something they need to take charge of to retain some responsibility. For example, initiating a sitter service is a step in the right direction toward short-term respite care. Once short-term respite care is accepted and the carers are empowered by this provision, then the process of accepting care empowers their internal locus of control, and they (the carers, often parents) are beginning to regain their own identity. Possibly this might coincide with their disabled child reaching adolescence or the early stage of adult life. The result will be greater independence for the parents as their child reaches adulthood, and the transition from dependence to independence is potentially achieved. Families concerned for their disabled child, from my studies, may find such considerations difficult to deal with due to a sense of guilt and concerns that only they can really provide the needed care. Professionals may alleviate much of this distress by negotiating and handling the provision of the needed services on the family's behalf.

Family vulnerability

The families that were interviewed were varied in their response to external support (from professionals or from within the community) and some families seemed isolated from any form of professional support. In the latter type of family, parents did not acknowledge the caring role taken on by siblings and seemed reluctant to access professional support. These families seemed the most vulnerable in their isolation, really needing professional support to assist them. Perhaps it is a form of family pride not to seek help; perhaps this is a form of distrust displayed towards professionals who otherwise might provide support. It is possible that such reactions are due to some kind of uncertainty in revealing family difficulties when perceiving professionals as helpers. This may signify an admission that the family cannot manage, so the need for a service is refused, or avoided, and the position is maintained in order to retain a false mythology that all is fine and help is not required. In these circumstances the needs of the family are, in my view, likely to be greater than most.

Siblings

The needs of siblings should be considered equally with those of others in the family. Professional workers must seek to enable the inclusion of siblings within family discussions and in the offering of service options, such as membership of the siblings support group. Services for the siblings of children with disabilities should offer some form of compensatory activities combined with the opportunity to talk with others. In the siblings research, the support group illustrated how siblings may begin to help themselves when provided with a venue that is enabling of discussion and the sharing of feelings. However, not all children will welcome membership of such a group, and that 'right' has to remain their choice.

Common Assessment Framework (DfES 2006a)

This indicates the need to integrate and to focus attention on the needs of children and young people. The intent is to provide a standardised approach to the assessment of a child's needs and in determining how those needs should be met. This fits with a multi-agency partnership espoused in Burke (1993, p.169), indicating the need for closer working in partnerships with carers and professionals alike. Such a union is necessary to realise the scale of the services that are required to meet needs. Clearly early intervention is necessary, and in meeting needs an integrated family assessment is essential.

Assessment is more specifically about reporting on a service user's needs and finding ways of meeting those needs with the agreement of the families and professionals involved. However, if one is implementing an assessment framework regarding the needs of children, Bell and Wilson (2003) describe the necessity to work directly with children covering five areas. These are: seeing the child; observing; engaging with the child; talking and listening to the child; and undertaking shared activities. Errors in practice regarding the Victoria Climbié case (Laming 2003) identified missed opportunities to see the child; and as with a disabled child and the need for a sibling viewpoint, not involving the child precludes the possibility of a fully objective assessment.

A process model of assessment

Working with a child can be the outcome of assessment if a key working scheme is implemented following a broader based family assessment.

However, while the framework for assessing children with needs indicates that 'assessment is the first stage' (DoH 2000a, p.29), this excludes the process of identifying *why an assessment is required*. The first stage has to be the point of referral because the referral identifies the reason why some form of intervention is needed. An assessment without an indication of why it is necessary would be like going into surgery without having a reason for doing so. Assessment should follow the initial need identified by the referring agent; it may change but it is the starting point for all interventions and future assessments. It provides some insight into the difficulties faced by the child or family or both.

In my conception of assessment, a process model begins with a request for assistance, the point of referral, followed by the initial considerations by the practitioner of some form of action with the service user. This involves contact with the user and other professionals, and discussions on the nature of the problem (the assessment). The next step considers the making of plans to deal with difficulties and implementing them subject to an agreement by the parties involved. Finally, evaluating the success or otherwise of the assessment and involvement determines the type of outcome achieved. This process model can be served by the acronym RECIPE, which stands for Referral, Engagement, Contact with the user, Initial Plan and Evaluation. This extends the ASPIRE model (ASsessment, Planning, Interventions, and Review and Evaluation) which, like the assessment framework, seems to neglect the importance of the referral. It includes the referral stage from the beginning, recognising that the initial request for intervention is the starting place for any intervention.

Guidance from the Department for Education and Skills (DfES) (2003) indicates that the initial assessment of need should involve a coordination of multi-agency support for families, better information and access for families, improved professional knowledge and skills, and reviewing and developing of partnerships between the agencies involved. This is not greatly different from the suggestions by Burke and Cigno (1996, 2000).

Key working
The idea of a key worker is not particularly revolutionary but is still an area where families with disabled children need help to deal with the complexities of service provision. Needs-led services as discussed by Burke and Cigno (1996, p.37) were identified in the NHS and Com-

munity Care Act 1990, following Griffiths (1988) in the suggestion for a key worker. The lead professional, considered as necessary within the *Common Assessment Framework* (DfES 2006a and b), also indicates that key coordinating tasks should rest with one worker. Such help is still not always achievable, even though a single point of contact was clearly identified in the aftermath of the Green Paper, *Every Child Matters* (2003) in the need to provide information, to help obtain the services, and to assist with advocacy. Key workers consistently report positive effects on relationships with service users, with fewer unmet needs and a greater sense of family wellbeing.

Indeed, in Burke and Cigno (1996, p.37) the provision of directly helping families suggested a sequencing process for key working:

- support at an informal level through family friends and local resources

- preventive work to alleviate stress and strain on families

- service delivery work to access specific services

- coordinated services to avoid fragmentation and gaps in support

- an empowering style to enable families to gain control over their own requirements.

However, I would review this to suggest now that such a model is not so much needed as a sequential provision of services, as an overall fully embracing approach considering all possibilities from the outset in implementing an initial plan with the family. Essentially this is what a key worker service should be providing.

The overarching theme in this discussion is clearly the need for service provision via agency resources coordinated by a key worker or lead professional. Consequently, I will now re-examine the need for services based on my research.

The need for services
The framework for professional practice (DoH 2000a), as I have mentioned, is based on recognising the needs of families and of children in particular; in the case of siblings, the framework also has limitations in terms of identifying needs as a reflection of the family unit. My findings therefore have some general consequences for practice, for it is possible that some degree of professional neglect is more likely to be a

consequence of an assessment model that does not focus sufficiently on family members including siblings and the disabled child.

The assessment framework, in terms of needs within families with disabled children, is flawed in its construction due to its broad conceptual base (the breadth of family and environmental factors) and its central focus on an individual child in need (effectively excluding siblings). This may result in competing pressures to achieve tasks not necessarily related to the family's needs. Such pressures may result in missed areas of an otherwise 'full' assessment. The focus of assessment in families with disabled children needs to soften to the family as a unit, and that is where the family assessment should be located.

The family practitioner might give due regard to the following:

- Women carers featured predominantly as the primary carer of children with disabilities, regretting missed opportunities for 'other' job opportunities.

- Nearly three-quarters of families reported that they found it difficult to arrange outings as a whole family and tended to do things separately.

- Disability is not necessarily confirmed during infancy and the need for a diagnosis is a major issue for some families. A diagnosis makes little impact on siblings, who know their brother or sister rather than viewing the condition.

- Disabled children were positively regarded by over 70 per cent of families, and indications were that many family relationships were stronger consequently.

- Parents reported that over 40 per cent of children with disabilities needed 24-hour supervision. Parents spent a considerable time attending to 'hands-on' caring tasks.

- Service provision is associated with professional intervention. Without professional intervention families get less help.

- Families that tend not to contact professionals fail to have a knowledge base of available resources.

Service provision is varied, and possibly even avoided by those reporting little use of services. This poses the question: is being labelled a service user a stigmatising experience? Apparently so, and avoidance is understandable; but the cost to the family is that they miss out on support, which can only increase problems when parents are stressed in caring for a child with disabilities and when they have no one they can turn to. It takes a dedicated and sensitive professional to offer the help and assistance required without instilling a sense of patronage or extolling the exceptional 'packages of care' that have been provided, all of which are, after all, only representative of a family's entitlement.

It is clear that parents, siblings and the child with a disability need to vocalise their experience in seeking professional avenues of help. When parents adopt an excluding approach, expressed as 'We just get on with it', they do not necessarily recognise the needs of either their disabled or their non-disabled children. It is very clear that parental views might not accurately reflect the care role that siblings have, so that siblings are vulnerable when their contribution to the family is not recognised.

Parents should discuss situations openly with their non-disabled children. Professionals need this awareness also. Not to involve parents and siblings might unintentionally widen the gulf for the more isolated family, not just between family and professionals, but also within the family itself. In such circumstances, professional workers should distinguish between the expressed views of parents from those of children and young people in the family. This can only be done by talking to the young people concerned as reflected by this research. Including the views of young people is needed in an overarching family assessment which is then instrumental in providing the needed services.

Conclusion

The positive views expressed by children with disabilities and their families often balance the more negative opinions. There are many positives, in families strengthened by a united front, a greater awareness of others, and siblings sensitive to the needs of their parents and disabled brother or sister. Indeed disabled children will express their own desires, when included; but not necessarily verbally or in more conventional ways, but usually sufficient to be indicative of agreement or displeasure. However, positive outlooks can be dampened by the stress of inordinate caring duties and few opportunities for respite for the family. The resulting stress impacts on the whole family.

The cases examined in this book suggest a typified reaction by families to the continual adjustment to living with a disabled child. They develop response strategies to enable them to partake in social engagements, to achieve some coming to terms with the everyday experience of living with disability. Disability by association, as I have demonstrated, is real experience; it is how others treat people involved in the lives of disabled children, and it is why special provision is essential for the family with a disabled child. The process of helping has been mentioned, through assessment, support groups, through service involvement – and all needing the cooperation of the families and young people involved if it is to work. However, to make any progress the needs have to be recognised, and the person-centred model of disability and disability by association as a social construct helps that process, identifying individuals in the family and the family as a social unit as in need of social care. The sense of exclusion experienced by the most vulnerable families requires eradication through knowledge, training and professional understanding. In the end, it may be a matter of making greater efforts to work together for all the parties involved.

Practice notes

What is an assessment?

The process whereby a user's need for a support service is determined is called an assessment. This will often involve a report following consultation and a discussion with the user on the nature of services that are needed, based on the experience of the family and their expressed requirements. There may be a potential conflict between services that are desired and those that can be provided, and when there is disagreement, some element of dissatisfaction will be perceived by the service user. A lack of service resource should be acknowledged as unmet need and efforts should be made to meet the required provision where possible, otherwise the constraints of providing care for a disabled child will only be compromised, inducing unnecessary stress for all those concerned.

Does caring induce a degree of social exclusion?

The caring task may prompt a degree of social isolation when a service user does not ask for support services. When services are not sought it does not follow that services are not needed. Services may not be sought because they are not known about, or it may be due to uncertainty about the role of support workers in making service provision available. The implication is that services are not required and an assessment of need is therefore not necessary. Service availability needs to be well documented because the most isolated service users are often those who are the least demanding. Consequently, a proactive intervention style, adopted by the professional, is needed to assist these families. It is argued that a proactive role for social care providers is necessary to overcome the inequity, and experience of social exclusion, that might otherwise occur.

Will my disabled child ever achieve independence?

The impact of adjusting to caring for a disabled child entails an acceptance of disability, but that acceptance may confer an impression that caring must become a lifetime commitment. The reality is that many disabled people can achieve a degree of self-sufficiency or near to that, albeit some may need help with personal care. However, a parent having made an unconscious or stated commitment to lifelong care may find it difficult to let go of caring duties, perhaps when the child is near to adulthood and ought to have the opportunity to experience a degree of independence. The transition to independence is difficult for all concerned, but it should never be dismissed as impossible. Parents should not feel guilty if they can no longer retain the caring responsibilities themselves. The short answer is that disabled children grow up and have a right to a more independent life, a possibility most parents should be encouraged to consider, for their needs and for their child's, without the attachment of guilt or feelings of inadequacy. The reality is that parental contacts can remain in place which will ultimately enrich relationships beyond the strain of the former caring tasks.

Appendix

The Research Process

This appendix summarises the research methods adopted within the four studies that inform the text. The studies concern the need for family support, the needs of siblings of disabled children, and the needs of children with learning disabilities. The four research studies included a qualitative commentary to balance the survey data, on how those involved perceived their lives from their perspective of living with disability. Collectively these studies underpin the findings reported and examined in this book.

The research

The relationship between the research investigations is shown in Figure A.1, which identifies the vantage point of the studies regarding family members, parents, the disabled child and siblings. The first study was on the need for family support. The second and third were comparative, at different periods, concerning the relationship between brothers and sisters and their disabled siblings. The fourth was about the experience of young people who attended a group for young people with special needs. The commonality of all four studies is represented as the core family identity, and the sense is that disability belongs not only to the child with a disability, but also to all family members.

These four studies viewed the diagnosis of a child as being disabled or with special needs as a significant event in family life, requiring a greater level of understanding, particularly concerning the social impact of disability. Disability itself is considered to represent a broad spectrum of need and individual concerns in what might be thought of as 'disability in the family'. The families involved in the studies had with their sons and daughters encountered disability as a medical labelling process, one that ascribes a condition to the child, which has significance in terms of education, social and future expectation for that child. Figure A.1 reflects the field research undertaken to explore the varying aspects of family

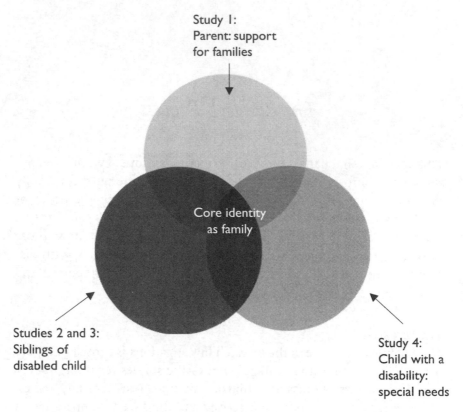

Study 1:
Parent: support
for families

Core identity
as family

Studies 2 and 3:
Siblings of
disabled child

Study 4:
Child with a
disability:
special needs

Figure A.1 Family interaction model reflecting the research strategy

experience, including the views expressed by parents, siblings and the child identified as disabled.

A detailed discussion of the methodology of each study will be found in the original research reports mentioned within the text. The methods will be reviewed in this Appendix. Despite the holistic approach to the research, it is not fully inclusive of all disability-related matters. For example, an area not examined concerns the need to understand how adults with disabilities are assisted (or not) in the care needs of their families; or, to give another example, how developing sexuality influences choices made for young people with disabilities.[1] The model shown in Figure A.1, while indicating that research was focused on family members, parents, child and siblings, does not reflect the fact that the questionnaires used (and discussed in terms of construction below) also incorporated themes relating to the nature of disability, services provided, and impact on the family more generally. In a sense, all the studies looked at family matters although each had a different initiating theme.

Some limitations to the studies

The respective definitions of disability and impairment, which may initiate specifically related research that reports on the impact of certain particular and diagnosed medical conditions, is not examined in this research. The intent here is not to debate the nature or type of disability; indeed a detailed classification of impairments is not provided, because a more generalised social understanding of disability as a family concern is required. Thus, disability is employed as a social construction to aid our understanding of how families respond to (and are responded to by) others in matters relating to the experience of living with a disabled child – including how the child central to the disability label feels and reacts. However, to understand the nature of disabling conditions, some elements of diagnosis are reported to show how comparable the groups are, especially when some degree of generalisation is helpful in a synthesis of the findings.

The research is biased somewhat owing to the regional nature of the work carried out. Also, the numbers of respondents do not compare with a full-scale national study, or even a total population study within regional catchments. This does not diminish these studies, but serves to indicate that what these families and young people had to say, what they felt, thought and experienced, is important because they are representative of other families with disabled children and a cross-section of views are recorded to balance the more quantitative data.

Population bases

The four survey samples were drawn from different locations, mostly within the North East of England.

- The first group included a total population from a special school and a sample population from a school with an integrated special unit.

- The second group was a sample population from the North East of England. In response terms, it was mainly representative of North East Lincolnshire.

- The third group was from an education facility for children with special needs in the Hull area.

- The fourth group included the total population of children attending a Children's Centre, identified as the Yorkshire group, plus, for comparative purposes, a small number of young people attending a similar group in the London area.

The sampling process was intended to be representative of groups and settings relating to the needs of families with disabled children. Indeed, it is argued that the needs for sampling procedures as identified by Denzin and Lincoln (1994, p.202), when studies should be representative of experiences that are likely to occur, is generally reflective of the methodology followed in these studies.

Representation

The issue of how representative these studies are of differing parts of the UK is not fully addressed, although the studies are collectively representative of a comprehensive review over a period exceeding ten years. The data from each respondent are individually based and no respondent appears twice, although there was a limited three-year follow-up to the second study to identify how families reported in Burke and Cigno (1996) had fared subsequent to that study. The studies are effectively a generalised snapshot of family experiences and a longitudinal element to the studies is not included for the most part. However, given the breadth of the studies the effect is of triangulating, as defined by Flick (1998, p.230), such that the findings improved the depth and range of the field work and enabled consistency in the methods employed.

Ethical considerations

The process of undertaking research can appear straightforward if considered to involve simply asking a number of questions and reporting the results. Unfortunately the process is more complex than that, although some very useful information may be gleaned by asking a series of standard questions to gain a view about a particular interest or area of inquiry. The realities of social research have developed a specific methodology. In all four studies undertaken to inform a holistic family view of childhood disability, the need for ethical considerations necessitated seeking, in the first place, permissions from the University of Hull's ethical committee.

The methodologies described in the outline below had to be approved by a committee with an independent input to ensure that work which involved talking to families and children was protective of their needs, enabling those involved to agree, disagree or to question the process which required their involvement. Reporting of results had to respect the confidential nature of any interviews and personal information held on interviewees. This necessarily reflects back on the researchers, who needed to be identified as suitable people to do the research, qualified to do so and of good character.

Criminal Records Bureau checks were necessary to ensure that those undertaking the research would not place a child at risk, even though the researchers, as academic staff of a university, were also qualified professionals within the field of social care. These checks on the researchers' background, plus the approvals that were required before the research could be undertaken, which followed ethical guidelines set by organisations like the British Sociological Association and utilised by Hull University to ensure that areas of inquiry were legitimate given the nature of the study. That is, the research is designed to improve knowledge from a social science perspective and would offer some insight into the situations examined.

Recommendations, outlined by Grinyer (2002), concern the consequences of fieldwork research participants, and indicate that issues of moral judgements are not context free. There are ethical considerations involved when talking to children about their needs, wishes and feelings (Beresford 1997). This is especially the case when the population to be interviewed have varying degrees of 'special needs' or are related to children with disabilities. Malin and Wilmot (2000) report on the need for a 'balance' between decisions that might cause a conflict with 'client autonomy against client protection' (p.223). It is important to realise that the professional relationship is in a potential state of conflict when attempting to respect the confidential nature of reported information that could, if identifying protection issues, put the researcher into the position of referral to a professional agency.

This challenge is also apparent in other ways. It is the commonly accepted view that research participants should not be identified, but an issue arises when protecting the participant endangers another (see also Gorard 2002). This leaves the researcher with a sense that the anonymity of the subject might not always be guaranteed. The debate around these issues also concerns children with disabilities and special needs when their continued experience is that others decide the balance between risk they may take and their individual autonomy, which may be an experience through to their adult life. There is, therefore, some merit in thinking about how this balance is handled with such young people, between confidentiality, individual autonomy and parental responsibility, and especially the input a researcher has when making an investigative study.

Fortunately the research did not present any such conflict. However, as all the researchers were professionally qualified in social care, on a number of occasions families were clearly seeking some form of support which raised issues about becoming involved and offering advice as professional workers rather than maintaining a distance as academic researchers. In all such matters, respondents were encouraged to refer back to the professional agencies with which they had contact.

Once the methodologies were agreed and research staff were cleared to undertake interviews involving parents and children, it was necessary to ensure that parents and their children agreed to the research process. This involved completing interviews with families, and in accordance with concerns of the type raised by Ramcharan and Cutcliffe (2001), acknowledged that acceptance to undertake research interviews (by parents and children) could be withdrawn at any time. This meant that the decision, for example, to interview a child required an acceptance to do so between parents and child, to enable the interview to proceed, but that the interviews could be ended for any reason if those involved, including the researcher, thought any element of distress or reluctance to continue was evident.

Our families were specifically concerned with diagnosis of disability, and its continuing impact on family life. A systematic methodology and protocol pertinent to the research had to be followed, resulting in a similarity of research design across all four studies, as explained below.

General design

The general research design was similar for all four studies. It is noted, however, that these studies were conducted with diverse population groupings, so questionnaires were returned by different respondents. Questionnaires used in all four studies were similar, following the format suggested by an original pilot study reported in Burke and Cigno (1996) and from sibling studies by Burke and Montgomery (2000, 2001). Only the third sibling study did not include a pilot stage because it replicated the main stage of study two. The general research design had a basic overlay as represented schematically in Figure A.2, which is a simplification of the design shown in Burke (2004, p.36).

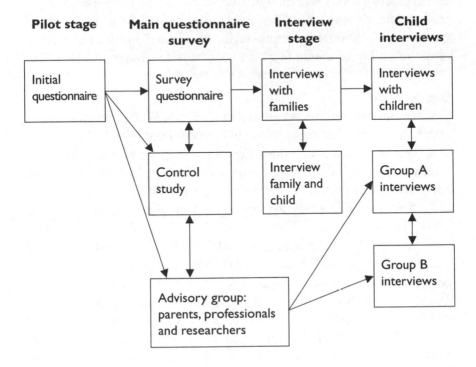

Figure A.2 General research design

Stages

Each study was conducted in four stages: a pilot (excluded in the third study), a main stage based on family completed questionnaires, a third stage involving interviews with parents, and a final stage involving interviews with children at home or in a group location.

In the first study a group location for interviewing young people was not available and had not been part of the original research design. In subsequent studies this omission was remedied (as represented in Figure A.2) following suggestions from an advisory group involving parents and professional social care workers. Two group locations were used in interviewing young people: one involved a group of siblings of disabled children (the second and third study on siblings), while the second involved a special needs group (the fourth study on special needs research).

The main stage of each study had a control group of families not involved in the main group and invariably these included follow-up family interviews. The siblings study initially reported in Burke and Montgomery (2003) was followed up in the study by Burke and Fell (2007); and although the first sibling study also had a small control group, the follow-up study improved the data initially generated in terms of the reliability of the findings, an issue raised in Burke (2004, p.40).

Questionnaires

Research instruments are according to Corbetta (2003, p.82) designed to enable the areas for investigation to be completed reliably. This means that questions asked have to have meaning for the respondent. This was determined by including sections on the disabled child, family members, questions on the impact of disabilities, contacts with helping agencies, and a final section seeking agreement for follow-up interviews (Burke 2004, p.131).

The questionnaire was designed with both open-ended and closed questions (Polgar and Thomas 1991). The first type were to elicit a general response, such as 'What positive benefit has having a child with a disability brought to your life?' Although this required a positive view which is 'forced', it enabled an identification with the respondent's own set attitudes concerning the benefits of living with disability. The closed questions limited choice to fixed categories, some listed in terms of services received, others being self-identified such as the nature of disability, sex and age. The self-completed questionnaire was also used as a basis for interviewing parents, checking the original answers and enabling elaboration on points raised.

Each family was sent a self-completion questionnaire during the main stage of the research. A question was included to request permission to gain access to the family, with a further question to request permission to interview children within the family (Burke 2004, p.131). Children and young people were not interviewed without the agreement of the families, and the children themselves could withdraw from the interview if they so wished, even if this was at the point of undertaking the interview. Only one family refused to participate after initially agreeing to the interview, and the matter ended at that point without further discussion.

Interviews with children followed an open-ended format (Burke 2004, p.137) and the interviewer introduced general areas for discussion. This is an interview process which, according to Silverman (2000) provides a deeper understanding of social experiences. The process was essentially similar to that explained in Burke (2005, p.365), including questions of the type related to sibling group attendance, such as 'What is the best part of going to a group?' This positive question was followed by a negative one, 'What is the worst part of going to a group?', to ensure a balanced approach and to encourage further comments. However, these interviews were only semi-structured, so they depended on the inherent skills of the researchers as professionals in social work or as counsellors.

Interviewers were acquainted with the need to 'break the ice' (Edwards and Talbot 1999) when dealing with families and children. It is mentioned in Chapter 1 that children are often singled out as different by virtue of race, gender or disability, so understanding the home and circumstances is a vitally important part of understanding the child and his or her expressed views. The children's views contributed to this examination and helped in providing an understanding of disability discrimination in the form of social exclusion. However, involving the child in a research study also has its particular problems, as discussed above.

The status of the researchers as social care professionals also suggested a case history approach to recording the interactions with the interviewees. This produced material of a qualitative type to complement the quantitative data resulting from the survey material.

Study population
Table A.1 shows the responses from the four studies, and Figure A.3 is a graphical depiction. These show the number of families that completed the questionnaires, usually the parents, but in a few cases it was evident that a foster carer was involved. Sixty-seven families returned questionnaires in the first study, 56 and 60 in the second and third and 30 families in the fourth study, with 213 families in total representing 215 children with disabilities (two families with two disabled children in this sample). The response rates (i.e. the proportion completing the questionnaires out of the number of questionnaires initially distributed) were 70 per cent (67 out of 96), 68 per cent (41 out of 60 in the main stage of the research) and 12.2 per cent (60 out of 499), and 100 per cent (30 out of 30) from the special needs group. The low response rate in the third study was due to distribution of the questionnaires by agencies more

remote to the research base. Nevertheless, the populations were representative of the area or group selected in three out of four studies.

Interestingly, the second study featured respondents with siblings attending a siblings support group (and included a control group study where siblings did *not* attend a support group), contrasting with the third study where siblings did not attend a support group, meaning that siblings were representative of those with group support and those without group support. The majority of siblings (73%) attended a support group in the second study contrasted with a similar proportion (75%) not attending a support group in the third study; in a sense, the proportions were reversed. In the latter, as a replication study, it was interesting to note that despite the substantial variation in the response rates, the findings from studies two and three had major similarities. In particular, results reported in Chapter 6 concerning the roles of siblings in the family and activities in which families engaged all helped with an increased confidence in the representation achieved by the returned questionnaires in the final study.

Table A.1 Responses

	Number of families	Number of children
Study 1*	67	67
Study 2	56	177
Study 3	60	167
Study 4*	30	30

*Brothers and sisters were excluded from reported results.

Sibling studies

Only studies two and three produced data on siblings, and these data were omitted from the first and fourth studies. Consequently Table A.1 shows studies one and four as only representing the child with a disability and not the number of siblings in the family. This is addressed in studies two and three where, in total, 116 families provided data and had between them 344 children (aged from birth to 32 years). There were 118 children with disabilities (aged 2 to 20 years), and two families with two disabled children. Interviews followed a selection of representative respondents from each survey, including 37 children who were seen at home and 16 who participated in group interviews at a Children's

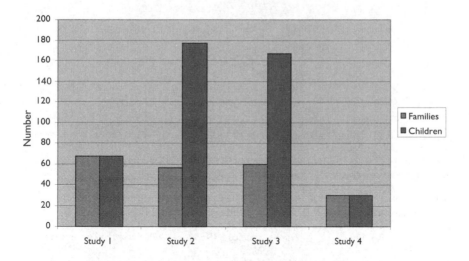

Figure A.3 The results from Table A.1

Centre. The female to male ratio of siblings was approximately two girls to one boy in the first survey returns (matching the national estimate by the ESRC in 2006) and one to one in the second study (excluding larger sibling families). No specific differences were identified due to the sex of the sibling. It had been speculated that girls would be more often cast in a caring role following results from the first survey, although there was not any apparent difference in the second study.

Conclusion

A substantial amount of material was gathered and this is reflected in the analysis in the chapters of this book. Analysis of the findings was by SPSS for studies one to three, and hand extraction of data on the fourth evaluative study. Interviews were written up as case reports and much attention has been given to recount views expressed by carers, mostly parents, their siblings, and children identified as having 'special needs' to represent children with disabilities. It is intended that the voice of families should come across in this book, to represent their needs and experiences of service delivery and social engagements.

Note

1   Exceptionally the case of Ashley X mentioned in Chapter 1 does raise this issue, but in the context of who made the decision to operate on her and for what purpose.

References

Abercrombie, N., Hill, S. and Turner, B. S. (2000) *The Penguin Dictionary of Sociology*, 4th edn. London: Penguin.

Adams, R. (1996) *Social Work and Empowerment*. London: Macmillan.

Aldridge, J. and Becker, S. (1994) *A Friend Indeed: The Case for Befriending Young Carers*. Loughborough: Young Carers Research Group, Loughborough University.

Atkinson, R. L., Atkinson, R. C., Smith, E. E., Bem, D. J. and Hilgard, E. R. (1990) *Introduction to Psychology*, 10th edn. Orlando, FL: Harcourt Brace Jovanovich.

Ayres, C. (2007) 'Parents defend decision to keep girl a child.' *Times Online*. www.timesonline.co.uk/tol/news/article1289216.ece (accessed 16 November 2007).

Baldwin, S. and Carlisle, J. (1994) *Social Support for Disabled Children and their Families: A Review of the Literature*. Edinburgh: HMSO.

Balter, L. and Tamis-LeMonda, C. (2003) *Child Psychology*. East Sussex: Psychology Press.

Banks, J. A. (1991) *Teaching Strategies for Ethnic Studies*. Needham Heights, MA: Allyn & Bacon.

Barnes, C. and Mercer, G. (2003) *Disability*. Cambridge: Polity Press.

Barr, H. (1999) 'Genetic counselling: a consideration for the potential and key obstacles to assisting parents adapting to a child with learning disabilities.' *British Journal of Learning Disabilities 17*, 30–36.

Baxter, C., Cummins, R. A. and Yiolitis, L. (2000) 'Parental stress attributed to family members with and without disability: a longitudinal study.' *Journal of Intellectual & Developmental Disability 25*, 2, 105–118.

BBC News (2007a) 'Q&A: special educational needs.' http://news.bbc.co.uk/1/hi/education/6241691.stm (accessed 16 November 2007).

BBC News (2007b) 'Autism "more common than thought".' http://news.bbc.co.uk/1/hi/health/5174144.stm (accessed January 2007).

BBC News, Education (2007a) 'Behaviour problems strain schools'. http://news.bbc.co.uk1/hi/education/3734370.stm (accessed January 2007).

BBC News, Education (2007b) 'Special education policy "a disaster".' http://news.bbc.co.uk/1/hi/education/3630387.stm (accessed January 2007).

Bednar, R. L. and Kaul, T. J. (1994) 'Experimental group research: can the cannon fire?' In A. E. Bergin and S. L. Garfield (eds) *Handbook of Psychotherapy and Behaviour Change*. New York, NY: Wiley.

Bell, M. and Wilson, K. (eds) (2003) *The Practitioner's Guide to Working with Families*. Basingstoke: Palgrave.

Beresford, B. (1994) 'Support from services.' In B. Beresford, *Positively Parents: Caring for a Severely Disabled Child*. HMSO: London.

Beresford, B. (1995) *Expert Opinions: A National Survey of Parents Caring for a Severely Disabled Child*. Bristol: Policy Press.

Beresford, B. (1997) *Personal Accounts: Involving Disabled Children in Research*. The Stationery Office, Norwich: Social Policy Research Unit.

Beresford, B. (2003) 'The community equipment needs of disabled children and their families.' In *Research Works*, 2003-1. University of York, York: Social Policy Research Unit.

Beresford, B., Sloper, P., Baldwin, S. and Newman, T. (1996) *What Works in Services for Families with a Disabled Child*. Ilford: Barnardo's.

Blackard, M. K. and Barsch, E. T. (1982) 'Parents' and professionals' perceptions of the handicapped child's impact on the family.' *Journal of the Association of the Severely Handicapped 7*, 2, 62–72.

Bone, M. and Meltzer, H. (1989) *The Prevalence of Disability Among Children.* London: Office of Population Censuses and Surveys.

Bowlby, J. (1951) *Maternal Care and Mental Health.* Geneva: WHO.

Britton, C. (2001) *Telling It How It Is: Researching the Family's Perspective – What Is It Really Like for Families Managing their Child's Serious Condition at Home?* Birmingham: Handsel Trust.

Burke, P. (1991) 'Best of Both Worlds.' *Social Work Today 22*, 39, 18–9.

Burke, P. (1993) 'Oppressive and child disability.' In G. Bradley and K. Wilson (eds) *The State, the Family, and the Child.* Hull: Department of Social Policy and Professional Studies, University of Hull.

Burke, P. (1998) 'Children with severe learning disabilities.' In K. Cigno and D. Bourn (eds) *Cognitive–Behavioural Social Work Practice.* Aldershot: Arena.

Burke, P. (1999) 'Social service staff: risks they face and their dangerousness to others.' In P. Parsloe (ed) *Risk Assessment in Social Care and Social Work,* pp.107–118. London: Jessica Kingsley Publishers.

Burke, P. (2004) *Brothers and Sisters of Disabled Children.* London: Jessica Kingsley Publishers.

Burke, P. (2005) 'Listening to young people with special needs: the influence of group activities.' *Journal of Intellectual Disabilities 9*, 4, 359–376.

Burke, P. (2007) 'Disadvantage and stigma: a theoretical framework for associated conditions.' In P. Burke and J. Parker (eds) *Social Work and Disadvantage: Addressing Issues of Stigma through Association.* London: Jessica Kingsley Publishers.

Burke, P. and Cigno, K. (1995) *Children with Learning Disabilities and the Need for Family Support Networks.* Hull: The Children's Research Fund and Hull University.

Burke, P. and Cigno, K. (1996) *Support for Families: Helping Children with Learning Disabilities.* Aldershot: Ashgate.

Burke, P. and Cigno, K. (2000) *Learning Disabilities in Children.* Oxford: Blackwell Science.

Burke, P, and Cigno, K. (2001) 'Communicating with children with learning disabilities: recognising the need for inclusive practices.' *Journal of Child Centred Practice 6*, 2, 115–126.

Burke, P. and Fell, B. (2007) 'Childhood disabilities and disadvantage: family experiences.' In P. Burke and J. Parker (eds) *Social Work and Disadvantage: Addressing Issues of Stigma through Association.* London: Jessica Kingsley Publishers.

Burke, P. and Montgomery, S. (2000) 'Siblings of children with disabilities: a pilot study.' *Journal of Learning Disability 4*, 3, 227–236.

Burke, P. and Montgomery, S. (2001) 'Brothers and sisters: supporting the siblings of children with disabilities.' *Practice, Journal of the British Association of Social Workers 13*, 1, 25–34.

Burke, P. and Montgomery, S. (2003) *Finding a Voice.* Birmingham: Ventura Press.

Burke, P. and Parker, J. (2007) *Social Work and Disadvantage: Addressing Issues of Stigma through Association.* London: Jessica Kingsley Publishers.

Burke, P., Manthorpe, J. and Cigno, K. (1997) 'Relocating prevention in practice.' *Journal of Learning Disabilities for Nursing, Health and Social Care 1*, 4, 176–80.

Carpenter, B. and Herbert, E. (1997) 'Fathers: are we meeting their needs?' In B. Carpenter (ed) *Families in Context: Emerging Trends in Family Support and Early Intervention.* London: David Fulton.

Chamba, R., Ahmad, W., Hirst, M., Lawton, D. and Beresford, B. (1999) *On the Edge: Minority Ethnic Families Caring for a Severely Disabled Child.* York: Joseph Rowntree Foundation Policy Press.

Cigno, K. with Burke, P. (1997) 'Single mothers of children with learning disabilities: an undervalued group.' *Journal of Interprofessional Care 11*, 2, 177–186.

Clarke, H. (2006) *Preventing Social Exclusion of Children and Their Families.* Birmingham: Department of Education and Skills, University of Birmingham.

Cleave, G. (2000) 'The Human Rights Act 1998: how will it affect child law in England and Wales?' *Child Abuse Review 9*, 394–402.

Connors, C. and Stalker, K. (2003) *The Views and Experiences of Disabled Children and their Siblings: A Positive Outlook.* London: Jessica Kingsley Publishers.

Corbetta, P. (2003) *Social Research.* London: Sage Publications.

Corey, G. (2004) *Theory and Practice of Group Counselling,* 6th edn. Belmont: Thomson Brooks Cole.

Craft, A. and Brown, H. (1994) 'Personal relationships and sexuality: the staff role.' In A. Craft (ed) *Practice Issues in Sexuality and Learning Disabilities.* London: Routledge.

Cross, S. B., Kaye, E. and Ratnofsky, A. C. (1993) *A Report on the Maltreatment of Children With Disabilities.* Washington, DC: National Center for Child Abuse and Neglect.

Crow, L. (1996) 'Including all of our lives.' In J. Morris (ed) *Encounters with Strangers: Feminism and Disability.* London: The Women's Press.

Dale, B. (1995) 'Creating answers.' In D. Meyer (ed) *Uncommon Fathers: Reflections on Raising a Child with a Disability.* Bethesda, MD: Woodbine House Inc.

Dalley, G. (1993) 'Familist ideology and possessive individualism.' In A. Beatie, M. Gott, L. Jones, and M. Sidell (eds) *Health and Wellbeing.* London: Macmillan.

Daniel, B., Wassell, S. and Gilligan, R. (1999) *Child Development for Child Care and Protection Workers.* London: Jessica Kingsley Publishers.

Denzin, N. K. (1992) 'Whose corner is it anyway?' *Journal of Ethnography 22,* 1, 120–135.

Denzin, N. K. and Lincoln, Y. S. (1994) *Handbook of Qualitative Research.* London: Sage.

DfES (Department for Education and Skills) (2001) *The Code of Practice on the Identification and Assessment of Special Educational Needs.* London: The Stationery Office.

DfES (Department for Education and Skills) (2003) *Together from the Start: Practical Guidance for Professionals Working with Disabled Children (Birth to Third Birthday) and Their Families.* www.everychildmatters.gov.uk/_files/854DD6EB3299A0082A381D3284673C0 4.pdf (accessed January 2007).

DfES (Department for Education and Skills) (2006a) *The Common Assessment Framework for Children and Young People: Every Child Matters.* www.everychildmatters.gov.uk/ deliveringservices/caf (accessed January 2007).

DfES (Department for Education and Skills) (2006b) *The Common Assessment Framework for Children and Young People: Practitioners' Guide. Integrated Working to Improve Outcomes for Children and Young People.* www.everychildmatters.gov.uk/_files/F71B9C32893 BE5D30342A28 96043C234.pdf (accessed April 2007).

Dies, R. R. (1992) 'The future of group therapy.' *Psychotherapy 29,* 1, 58–64.

Dobson, B. and Middleton, S. (1998) *Paying to Care: the Cost of Childhood Disability.* York: Joseph Rowntree Foundation.

DoH (Department of Health) (1998) *Modernising Social Services.* London: The Stationery Office.

DoH (Department of Health) (2000a) *Framework for the Assessment of Children in Need and their Families.* London: The Stationery Office.

DoH (Department of Health) (2000b) *A Quality Strategy for Social Care.* London: HMSO.

DoH (Department of Health) (2001a) *Planning with People: Towards a Person Centred Approach – Guidance for the Implementation Group.* London: HMSO.

DoH (Department of Health) (2001b) *Valuing People: A New Strategy for Learning Disability for the 21st Century.* London: The Stationery Office.

DoH (Department of Health) (2002) *Planning with people: Accessible Guide.* www.publications.doh.gov.uk/learningdisabilities/planning/htm (accessed December 2007).

DoH (Department of Health) (2004a) *National Service Framework for Children, Young People and Maternity Services: Disabled Children and Young People and Those with Complex Health Needs.* London: The Stationery Office.

DoH (Department of Health) (2004b) *Valuing People: Moving Forward Together.* London: The Stationery Office.

DoH (Department of Health) (2007) *Social Care.* www.dh.gov.uk/en/Policyandguidance/ Social Care/index/htm (accessed January 2007).

DWP (Department of Works and Pensions) (2006) 'Updated estimate of the numbers of disabled people including people with limiting longstanding illnesses, and their associated spending power.' www.dwp.gov.uk/mediacentre/pressreleases/2006/feb/drc-015-090206.asp (accessed January 2007).

Donald, T. and Jureidini, J. (2004) 'Parenting capacity.' *Child Abuse Review 13*, 5–17.

Dowling, M. (2000) *Young Children's Personal, Social and Emotional Development*. London: Sage.

DPI (1982) *Proceedings of the First World Congress*. Singapore: Disabled People's International.

Dyson, L. (1996) 'The experience of families of children with learning disabilities: parental stress, family functioning and sibling self-concept.' *Journal of Learning Disabilities 2*, 9, 280–286.

Dyson, L. (1997) 'Fathers and mothers of school age children with developmental disabilities: parental stress, family functioning and social support.' *American Journal of Mental Retardation 102*, 3, 267–279.

Edwards, A. and Talbot, R. (1999) *The Hard-pressed Researcher: A Research Handbook for the Caring Professions*. London: Longman.

Emerson, E. and Hatton, C. (2005) *The Socioeconomic Circumstances of Families Supporting a Child at Risk of Disability in Britain in 2002*. Lancaster University, Lancaster: Institute for Health Research. www.lancs.ac.uk/fass/ihr/publications/ericemerson/secchild-disability.pdf (accessed January 2007).

ESRC (2006) *Society Today – Disability in the UK*. www.esrcsocietytoday.ac.uk/ ESRCInfoCentre/facts/UK/index42.aspx? (accessed January 2007).

European Development Fund (2002) *Policy Paper: Development Cooperation and Disability*, DOC EDF 02/1. www.edf-feph.org (accessed January 2007).

Every Child Matters (2003) Green Paper Cm 5860. www.everychildmatters.gov.uk/_files/ EBE7EEAC90382663E0D5BBF24C99A7AC.pdf (accessed January 2007).

Every Child Matters (2006) *Support for Families of Disabled Children*. www.everychildmatters.gov.uk/socialcare/disabledchildren/support (accessed January 2007).

Falhberg, V. (1994) *A Child's Journey Through Placement*. London: BAAF.

Farnfield, S. (1998) 'The rights and wrongs of social work with children and young people.' In J. Cheetham and A. F. Kazi (eds) *The Working of Social Work*. London: Jessica Kingsley Publishers.

Fawcett, B. (2000) *Feminist Perspectives on Disability*. Harlow: Prentice Hall.

Fitton, P. (1994) *Listen to Me: Communicating the Needs of People with Profound Intellectual and Multiple Disabilities*. London: Jessica Kingsley Publishers.

Flick, U. (1998) *An Introduction to Qualitative Research*. London: Sage.

Fonagy, P., Steele, M., Steele, H., Higgitt, A. and Target, M. (1994) 'The theory and practice of resilience.' *Journal of Child Psychology and Psychiatry 35*, 2, 231–257.

Fortin, J. (2003) *Children's Rights and the Developing Law*, 2nd edn. London: Lexis Nexis.

Foucault, M. (1980) in Gordon, C. (ed.) *Michel Foucault: Power/Knowledge: Selected Interviews and Other Writings 1972–1977 by Michel Foucault*. Hemel Hempstead: Harvester Wheatsheaf.

Franklin, A. and Sloper, P. (2007) *Participation of Disabled Children and Young People in Decision-making Relating to Social Care*. York: DfES/Social Policy Research Unit.

French, S. (2004) '"Can you see the rainbow?" Roots of denial.' In J. Swain, V. Finkelstein, S. French and N. Oliver (eds) *Disabling Barriers: Enabling Environments*, 2nd edn. London: Sage/Open University.

Frude, N. (1991) *Understanding Family Problems: A Psychological Approach*. Chichester: Wiley.

Fyson, R. and Simons, K. (2003) 'Strategies for change: making *Valuing People* a reality.' *British Journal of Learning Disabilities 31*, 153–158.

Garrett, P. (2003) 'Swimming with dolphins: the assessment framework, New Labour and new tools for social work with children and families.' *British Journal of Social Work 33*, 441–463.

Gillespie-Sells, K. and Campbell, J. (1991) *Disability Equality Training Guide*. Hertford: CCETSW.

Gillman, M. (2004) 'Diagnosis and assessment in the lives of disabled people: creating potentials/limiting possibilities?' In J. Swain, V. Finkelstein, S. French and N. Oliver (eds) *Disabling Barriers: Enabling Environments*, 2nd edn. London: Sage /Open University.

Goffman, E. (1963) *Stigma: Notes on the Management of Spoiled Identity.* New York: Simon and Schuster.

Goffman, E. (1974) *Frame Analysis: An Essay in the Organisation of Experience.* Penguin: London.

Goodley, D. (2000) *Self-advocacy in the Lives of People with Learning Difficulties.* Buckingham: Open University Press.

Goodley, D. (2005) 'Empowerment, self-advocacy and resilience.' *Journal of Intellectual Disabilities 9*, 4, 333–343.

Gorard, S. (2002) 'Ethics and equity: pursuing the perspective of non-participants.' *Social Research Update 39*, 1–5.

Graham, H. and Power, C. (2004) *Childhood Disadvantage and Adult Health: A Lifecourse Framework.* London: Health Development Agency website www.hda.nhs.uk/evidence (accessed November 2007).

Griffiths, E. (2002) *Social Work Practice with Disabled Children: The Experience of Five Families.* Norwich: University of East Anglia.

Griffiths, R. (1988) *Community Care: Agenda for Action.* London: HMSO.

Griggs, L. (2000) 'Assessment in community care.' In M. Davies (ed) *Blackwell Encyclopaedia of Social Work*, p.22. Oxford: Blackwell Science.

Grinyer, A. (2002) 'The anonymity of research participants: assumptions, ethics and practicalities.' *Social Research Update 36*, 1–4.

Hartrey, L. and Wells, J. S. G. (2003) *Special Brothers and Sisters: Stories and Tips for Siblings of Children with Special Needs, Disability or Serious Illness.* London: Jessica Kingsley Publishers.

Hendy, N. and Pascall, G. (2001) *Disability and Transition to Adulthood: Achieving Independent Living.* York: Joseph Rowntree Foundation.

Holdsworth, L. (1991) *Empowerment Social Work with Physically Disabled People.* Norwich: Social Work Monographs.

Hopson, B. (1981) 'Transitions, understanding and managing personal change.' In M. Herbert (ed) *Psychology for Social Workers.* London: Macmillan.

Houston, S. (2002) 'Re-thinking a systemic approach to child welfare: a critical response to the framework for the assessment of children in need and their families.' *European Journal of Social Work 5*, 301–312.

Howard, M. (1999) *Enabling Government: Joined-up Policies for a National Disability Strategy* (Fabian Society Discussion Paper 48). London: Fabian Society.

Hudson, B., Dearey, M. and Glendinning, C. (2005) *A New Vision for Adult Social Care: Scoping Services Users' Views.* University of York, York: Social Policy Research Unit.

Jack, G. (1997) 'An ecological approach to social work with children and families.' *Children and Family Social Work 2*, 109–120.

Jackson, S. (2000) 'Assessment in child care.' In M. Davies (ed) *Blackwell Encyclopaedia of Social Work.* Oxford: Blackwell Science.

Jenkinson, J. C. (1998) 'Parent choice in the education of students with disabilities.' *International Journal of Disability, Development and Education 45*, 189–202.

Jones, C. (1998) 'Early intervention: the eternal triangle.' In C. Robinson and K. Stalker (eds) *Growing Up with Disabilities.* London: Jessica Kingsley Publishers.

Joseph Rowntree Foundation (1999) *Supporting Disabled Children and their Families.* York: JRF.

Katz, S. W. (1975) *Creativity in Social Work.* Philadelphia, PA: Temple University Press.

Knight, A. (1996) *Caring for a Disabled Child.* London: Straightforward Publishing Ltd.

Laming, H. (2003) *The Victoria Climbié Inquiry Report, Cm 5730.* London: The Stationery Office. www.victoria-climbie-inquiry.org.uk (accessed December 2007).

Lazarus, R. and Foulkman, S. (1984) *Stress, Appraisal, and Coping.* New York: Springer.

Lefcourt, H. M. (1976) *Locus of Control: Current Trends in Theory and Research.* Hillsborough, NJ: Lawrence Erlbaum.

Lewis, A. (1995) *Children's Understanding of Disability.* London: Routledge.

Malin, N. A. and Wilmot, S. (2000) 'An ethical advisory group in a learning disability service: what they talk about.' *Journal of Learning Disabilities 4*, 3, 217–226.

Mayhew, K. and Munn, C. (1995) 'Siblings of children with special needs.' *Child Care in Practice 2*, 1, 30–38.

McNally, S., Bne-Shlomo, Y. and Newman, S. (1999) 'The effects of respite care on informal carers' well-being: a systematic review.' *Disability and Rehabilitation 21*, 1, 1–14.

McNair, J. and Rusch, R. (1991) 'Parent involvement in transition programs.' *Mental Retardation 29*, 2, 93–101.

Meyer, D. J. and Vadsey, P. F. (1997) *Sibshops: Workshop for Siblings of Children with Special Needs*, 2nd edn. Baltimore, MD: Paul H. Brooks.

Middleton, L. (1999) *Disabled Children: Challenging Social Exclusion.* Oxford: Blackwell Science.

Mirfin-Veitch, B., Bray, A. and Watson, M. (1997) '"We're just that sort of family": intergenerational relationships in families including children with disabilities.' *Family Relations 46*, 3, 305–311.

Mitchell, W. and Sloper, P. (2000) *User-friendly Information for Families with Disabled Children: A Guide to Good Practice.* York: Joseph Rowntree Foundation.

Morris, J. (1996) *Accessing Human Rights: Disabled Children and the Children Act.* Barkingside: Barnardo's.

Morris, J. (1998) *Encounters with Strangers.* London: The Women's Press.

Morris, J. (1999) 'Disabled children, child protection systems and the Children Act 1989.' *Child Abuse Review 8*, 2, 91–108.

Morris, J. (2001) *That Kind of Life.* London: Scope.

Murray, P. (2000) 'Disabled children, parents and professionals: partnership on whose terms?' *Disability and Society 15*, 4, 683–698.

Myers, R. (1978) *Like Normal People.* New York: McGraw-Hill.

National Statistics (2004) *The Health of Children and Young People.* www.statistics.gov.uk/Children/downloads/disability.pdf (accessed January 2007).

Naylor, A. and Prescott, P. (2004) 'Invisible children? The need for support groups for siblings of disabled children.' *British Journal of Special Education 31*, 4, 199–206.

Oldman, C. and Beresford, B. (1998) *Homes Unfit for Children: Housing Disabled Children and their Families.* Parsonage Green: Policy Press in association with the Joseph Rowntree Foundation and Community Care Magazine.

Oliver, M. (1990) *The Politics of Disablement.* London: Routledge Kegan Paul.

Oliver, M. (1996) *Understanding Disability: From Theory to Practice.* Basingstoke: Macmillan.

Oliver, M. and Barnes, C. (1998) *Disabled People and Social Policy: From Exclusion to Inclusion.* London: Longman.

Oliver, O. and Sapey, B. (2006) *Social Work with Disabled People.* Hampshire: Palgrave Macmillan.

Östman, M. and Kjellin, L. (2002) 'Psychological factors in relatives of people with mental illness.' *British Journal of Psychiatry 18*, 1, 494–498.

Parker, G. and Olsen, R. (1995) 'A sideways glance at young carers', paper delivered at a conference organised by the Social Services Inspectorate in Leicester, 27 June (reproduced in SSI (1995) *Young Carers: Something to Think About*, Department of Health).

Payne, S., Horn, S. and Relf, M. (2000) *Loss and Bereavement.* Buckingham: Open University Press.

Penn, H. (2005) *Understanding Early Childhood.* Buckingham: Open University Press.

Phillips, R. (1998) 'Disabled children in permanent substitute families.' In C. Robinson and K. Stalker (eds) *Growing Up with Disability: Research Highlights in Social Work 34.* London: Jessica Kingsley Publishers.

Pitkeathley, J. (1995) 'Pushed to the limits.' *Community Care*, 25–31 May, p.2.

Polgar, S. and Thomas, S. J. (1991) *Introduction to Research in the Health Sciences*, 2nd edn. Edinburgh: Churchill Livingstone.

Powell, M. (2001) 'New Labour and the Third Way.' *Critical Social Policy 20*, 39–60.

Powell, T. and Gallagher, P. (1993) *Brothers and Sisters: A Special Part of Exceptional Families.* Baltimore, MD: Brookes.

Powell, T. and Ogle, P. (1995) *Brothers and Sisters: A Special Part of Exceptional Families.* Baltimore, MD: Brookes.

Ramcharan, P. and Cutcliffe, J. (2001) 'Judging the ethics of qualitative research.' *Health and Social Care in the Community 9*, 6, 358–366.

Rapoport, L. (1970) 'Crisis intervention as a mode of brief treatment.' In R.W. Roberts and R. H. Nee (eds) *Theories of Social Casework.* Chicago, IL: University of Chicago Press.

Read, J. (2000) *Disability, the Family and Society: Listening to Mothers.* Buckingham: Open University Press.

Riva, M. T. and Kalodner, C. R. (1997) 'Group research: encouraging a collaboration between practitioner and research.' *Journal for Specialists in Group Work 22*, 4, 266–276.

Russell, P. (1997) '"Don't Forget Us". Children with Learning Disabilities and Severe Challenging Behaviour.' Report of a committee set up by the Mental Health Foundation. London: MH.

Rutter, M. (1981) *Maternal Deprivation Reassessed*, 2nd edn. Harmondsworth: Penguin.

Sable, P. (1989) 'Attachment, anxiety and loss of husband.' *American Journal of Orthopsychiatry 59*, 4, 550–556.

Scott, R. A. (1969) *The Making of Blind Men.* New York: Sage.

Scott, G., Campbell, J. and Brown, U. (2002) 'Child care, social exclusion and urban regeneration.' *Critical Social Policy 22*, 4, 226–246.

Seligman, M. (1991) *The Family With a Handicapped Child: Understanding and Treatment*, 2nd edn. New York, NY: Grune & Stratton.

Shakespeare, T. (2006) *Disability Rights and Wrongs.* Oxford: Routledge.

Shakespeare, T. and Watson, N. (2002) 'The social model of disability: an outdated ideology?' *Research in Social Science and Disability 2*, 9–28.

Shakespeare, T., Barnes, C., Priestley, M., Cunninghambirley, S., Davis, J. and Watson, N. (1999) *Life as a Disabled Child: A Qualitative Study of Young People's Experience and Perspectives.* University of Leeds: Disability Research Unit.

Shattock, P. and Whiteley, P. (2005) *The Changing Prevalence of Autism?* Autism Research Unit, University of Sutherland. http://osiris.sunderland.ac.uk/autism/incidence.htm (accessed October 2006).

Siegal, B. and Silverstein, S. C. (1994) *What About Me? Growing Up with a Developmentally Disabled Sibling.* New York: Plenum.

Silverman, D. (2000) *Doing Qualitative Research: A Practical Handbook.* London: Sage.

Smith, J. (2002) *Listening, Hearing and Responding: Core Principles for the Involvement of Children and Young People.* Department of Health, 20 June. www.dh.gov.uk/en/ Publicationsand statistics/Publications/PublicationsPolicyAndGuidance/DH_4072061, accessed on 3 December 2007.

Sobsey, D., Wells, D., Lucardie, R. and Mansell, S. (1995) *Violence and Disability: An Annotated Bibliography.* Baltimore, MD: Brookes.

Stalker, K. and Connors, C. (2004) 'Children's perceptions of their disabled siblings: "She's different but it's normal for us".' *Children and Society 18*, 3, 218–230.

Stroebe, M., Stroebe, W. and Hansson, R. O. (1977) *Handbook of Bereavement: Theory, Research and Intervention.* Cambridge: Cambridge University Press.

Stroebe, M. and Schut, H. (1999) 'The dual-process model of coping with bereavement.' *Death Studies 23*, 197–224.

Sutton, C. (1994) *Social Work, Community Work and Psychology.* Leicester: British Psychological Society.

Sullivan, P. M. and Knutson, J. F. (2000) 'Maltreatment and disabilities: a population-based epidemiological study.' *Child Abuse & Neglect 24*, 1257–1273.

Swain, J., Finkelstein, V., French, S. and Oliver, N. (eds) (2004) *Disabling Barriers: Enabling Environments*, 2nd edn. London: Sage/Open University.

Taanila, A., Jarvelin, M. and Kookonen, J. (1998) 'Parental guidance and counselling by doctors and nursing staff: parents' views of initial information and advice for families with disabled children.' *Journal of Clinical Nursing 7*, 6, 505–511.

Thomas, C. (1999) *Female Forms: Experiencing and Understanding Disability*. Buckingham: Open University Press.

Thomas, M. and Pierson, J. (1995) *Dictionary of Social Work*. London: Collins Educational.

Thompson, N. (2001) *Anti-discriminatory Practice*, 3rd edn. Basingstoke: Macmillan.

Thurgate, C. and Warner, H. (2005) 'Living with disability: part I.' *Paediatric Nursing 17*, 10, 37–42.

Tozer, R. (1996) 'My brother's keeper? Sustaining sibling support.' *Health and Social Care in the Community 4*, 3, 177–181.

Trevithick, P. (2000) *Social Work Skills*. Buckingham: Open University Press.

Trotter, C. (1999) *Working with Involuntary Clients: A Guide to Practice*. London: Sage.

Trute, B. and Hiebert-Murphy, D. (2002) 'Family adjustment to childhood developmental disability: a measure of parent appraisal of family impacts.' *Journal of Paediatric Psychology 27*, 3, 271–280.

Twigg, J. (1989) 'Models of carers; how do social care agencies conceptualise their relationships with informal carers?' *Journal of Social Policy 18*, 53–56.

United Nations (1989) *The Convention on the Rights of the Child*. Geneva: United Nations Children Fund.

Utting, W. (1995) *Family and Parenthood: Supporting Families, Preventing Breakdown*. York: Joseph Rowntree Foundation.

Vaughn, S. and Schumm, J. S. (1995) 'Responsible inclusion for students with learning disabilities.' *Journal of Learning Disabilities 28*, 5, 264–270.

Walker, S. (2002) 'Positive intervention: an outline of some of the legal obligations of public authorities. The provision of personal social services to children and families.' *Representing Children 15*, 1, 21–39.

Ward, L., Mallett, R., Heslop, P. and Simons, K. (2003) 'Transition planning: how well does it work for young people with learning disabilities and their families?' *British Journal of Special Education 30*, 3, 132–137.

Werner, E. (1990) 'Protective factors and individual resilience.' In S. Meisels and J. Shonkoff (eds) *Handbook of Early Childhood Interventions*. Cambridge: Cambridge University Press.

West, S. (2000) *Just a Shadow? A Review of Support for the Fathers of Children with Disabilities*. Birmingham: Handsel Trust.

Westcott, H. (1991) 'The abuse of disabled children: a review of the literature.' *Child Care Health and Development 17*, 242–258.

Wing, L. and Potter, D. (2002) 'The epidemiology of autistic spectrum disorders: is the prevalence rising?' *Mental Retardation and Developmental Disability Research Review 8*, 3, 151–161. www.ncbi.nlm.nih.gov/entrez/query.fcgi?cmd=Retrieve&db=PubMed-&list_ uids=12216059&dopt=Abstract (accessed January 2007).

Winnicott, D. W. (1975) *Through Paediatrics to Psycho-analysis*. London: Hogarth.

Wolfensberger, W. (1998) *A Brief Introduction to Social Role Valorization. A High-order Concept for Addressing the Plight of Socially Devalued People, and for Structuring Human Services*, 3rd edn. New York, NY: Syracuse University.

Yang, H. and McMullen, M.B. (2003) 'Understanding the relationships among American primary-grade teachers and Korean mothers: the role of communication and cultural sensitivity in the linguistically diverse classroom.' *Early Childhood Research and Practice 5*, 1. http://ecrp.uiuc.edu/v5n1/yang.html (accessed August 2006).

Index